THE

FASB

The People,
the Process,
and the
Politics

The Robert N. Anthony/Willard J. Graham Series in Accounting

G P 89 00031

THE

FASB

The People,
the Process,
and the
Politics

Paul B. W. Miller, Ph.D., C.P.A.
Professor of Accounting
University of Utah

Rodney J. Redding, Ph.D., C.P.A.
Visiting Associate Professor of Accounting
Georgetown University

1988
Second Edition

Homewood, Illinois 60430

© RICHARD D. IRWIN, INC., 1986 and 1988

All rights reserved. No part of this publication may be
reproduced, stored in a retrieval system, or transmitted,
in any form or by any means, electronic, mechanical,
photocopying, recording, or otherwise, without the prior
written permission of the publisher.

This book was set in Times Roman by Western Interface, Inc.
The editors were Ron Regis, Frank S. Burrows, Jr., Ethel Shiell,
and Merrily D. Mazza.
The production manager was Irene H. Sotiroff.
Malloy Lithographing, Inc. was the printer and binder.

ISBN 0-256-06265-X

Library of Congress Catalog Card No. 87–81820

Printed in the United States of America

1 2 3 4 5 6 7 8 9 0 ML 5 4 3 2 1 0 9 8

To:
Diana, David, and Greg
and
Brenda, Mike, and Kim

FOREWORD

Creating a new independent organization to assume primary responsibility for establishing standards for financial reporting in the private sector of the United States was a unique undertaking. It started in March 1971 when Marshall S. Armstrong, then president of the American Institute of Certified Public Accountants (AICPA), appointed a group of seven distinguished individuals from public accounting, business, law, finance, and academe to study the establishment of accounting standards and to make recommendations for improving the process—a process that had been in the hands of the AICPA for nearly 40 years. The study group issued its report in March 1972, and one year later the Financial Accounting Standards Board (FASB) was in place, operating under the auspices of a freestanding foundation formed with the enthusiastic cooperation of five (later six) sponsoring professional organizations—a remarkable achievement.

With more than 14 years of standards setting under its belt, the FASB is today an established institution playing what is widely recognized as a vital role in the functioning of the capital markets of the United States. An understanding of the FASB and its work should be pertinent to a broad spectrum of individuals whose personal or professional interests are touched by some aspect of financial reporting.

Miller and Redding have endeavored to provide a vehicle for obtaining that understanding. They have described the institution and its process, provided a glimpse of the background and qualifications of some of the people involved, and presented their assessments and perceptions of some of the Board's work. The assessments and perceptions of other observers or of the active participants may differ from those of Miller and Redding. That is to be expected. I hope that this book will stimulate others to learn more about the FASB and its work and arrive at their own judgments about its past and future.

Robert T. Sprouse
Former Vice Chairman
Financial Accounting Standards Board

PREFACE

The overall goal of *The FASB: The People, the Process, and the Politics* is to pull back the veil of mystique that prevents many people from understanding an organization that is very important to the accounting profession and to the U.S. economy. Contrary to what many may think, the Financial Accounting Standards Board is not an aloof or impersonal institution; rather, it is a vibrant and dynamic entity consisting of ambitious, high-energy, enthusiastic, and intelligent **people**. It is also common to find misconceptions that suggest that the FASB uses rigid, lockstep procedures in going about its work; this image is also invalid because each project involves a specially designed and flexible application of some general steps to produce a unique **process**. Some also *who?* seem to think that standards-setting activity is simply a search for a "best" answer by a cold, logical analysis of the issues from an ivory tower; in fact, by its nature, standards setting is very much a matter of **politics**. We believe that the reader will be better off by understanding the role of these three important factors.

ORGANIZATION OF THE BOOK

The book starts with a **Prologue** that consists primarily of five articles from the business press about a new accounting issue: in-substance defeasances of debt. Through the articles, the reader can see the issue emerge, create trouble, attract attention from regulators, receive an authoritative resolution, and then be submitted to an after-the-fact analysis. The articles also reveal a number of points about the FASB and its process that are developed in later chapters.

    Chapter 1 lays a foundation for the rest of the book. It explains why financial accounting is considered to be important for the operation of the capital markets and for behavioral reasons. It also explains why there is an apparent need for accounting issues to be resolved authoritatively, and then describes why the FASB was formed and the sources of its authority. The chapter also considers the question of whether the Board is "political," and comes to the conclusion that it clearly is.

Chapter 2 examines the structure for setting standards that was originally suggested by the Wheat Study Group of the American Institute of Certified Public Accountants in 1972. It shows how this arrangement has been kept in tune with the times by both internal and external pressures. It is in this chapter that the **people** of the FASB are presented. We did not want to simply describe the positions in the FASB organization chart, but chose to also say something about the people who are filling those positions at the time the book goes into production. We also included a description of the Research and Technical Activities Staff duties and people, who often remain below the surface of more standard descriptions of the Board and its activities. An appendix to the chapter describes the FASB's two predecessor bodies and analyzes why they were replaced.

In **Chapter 3,** we describe the "due process" procedures by which the FASB searches for the right questions and the various possible answers. Because we were not hindered by space or other limitations, the chapter is able to go beyond the descriptions provided in the Board's own published materials and in standard accounting textbooks. We believe that the reader will be especially interested in two key points: (1) the **flexibility** inherent in the system that allows it to adapt to changes in the environment and factors unique to each project and (2) the **political wisdom** of having a due process that includes the different groups involved in standards setting. We are convinced that there is something new in the chapter for virtually everyone who reads it.

Chapter 4 represents a change of pace from the three preceding chapters, which focus on the Board and its activities. This chapter describes a series of accounting issues that have come before the Board and its predecessors over the years. Some of the issues must be resolved when they take on new forms in different transactions and industries; others reappear before the Board when there is dissatisfaction with the previous answer. We think that the discussions demonstrate how the structure described in the first three chapters has been brought to bear against real problems. We think that they also show how the Board's predecessors were somewhat handicapped by their structures and limited authority. Finally, we think they show clearly that the process for setting standards has always been **as much political as conceptual**.

Chapter 5 provides an especially in-depth view of the FASB's major (and highly controversial) effort to develop its **Conceptual Framework** for financial accounting and reporting. The analysis includes some inside views that were made possible by Paul's position as a faculty fellow on the Board's Staff during the controversial recognition and measurement phase. His membership on the Staff team gave him special insights into not only the issues that were discussed but also the personal and political pressures that significantly affected the outcome of the project. The chapter also includes a summary of the contents of each of the six existing Statements of Financial Accounting Concepts that is probably different from most of those provided elsewhere.

Finally, we conclude the book with an **Epilogue** that focuses on the future of the FASB. In doing so, it was important that we examine the **political** issues that surround the Board instead of merely looking at the technical issues that it must resolve. Thus, we look at the questions of whether standards setting should take place in the public or private sector, whether there exists a condition of standards overload or sufficient timely guidance, and whether the Board merely enjoys a high level of participation by financial statement preparers or is instead facing a serious problem of dominance by this group. We think that these questions are provocative but critical, and we think that we have addressed them realistically and thoroughly.

SUITABLE AUDIENCES

Because we are professional educators, it is only reasonable that we would aim this book at the instructional market. In particular, we think that college and university instructors will find this book a very useful supplement to their main textbooks for courses in Intermediate Accounting, Advanced Accounting, and Accounting Theory. We also think that it will have a place in graduate courses where the political nature of standards setting needs to be communicated to the students. In order to help instructors in these settings, we have included **questions** and **exercises** at the end of each chapter and the Epilogue that can be used to take students beyond a superficial reading of the material. We have also prepared an **Instructor's Manual** that includes answers to the questions and provides suggestions for conducting the class and using the exercises. The manual and a set of multiple choice examination questions are available without charge to those who adopt the book for classroom use.

Further, we think that this book is particularly suitable for continuing education for practicing accountants, regardless of whether they are engaged in public or private accounting. Many individuals in practice finished their formal education before the FASB came into existence or before it has become more widely recognized that standards setting is essentially a political process. By reading this book, they can understand much more about an important part of their professional environment and cope more easily with the changes that occur in it so persistently.

Like Lee Berton, who reviewed the first edition in *The Wall Street Journal,* we believe that the book is also useful for nonaccounting members of the business community who have to deal with accounting information, and who might wish to participate in the political processes of the FASB. In particular, we think that financial statement users will benefit especially from the material that is provided.

ACKNOWLEDGMENTS

In expressing appreciation for the efforts of others, we need to begin with the many people of the FASB who cooperated with us. They include the seven members of the Board who were serving in March 1987 (Denny Beresford, Vic Brown, Ray Lauver, David Mosso, Art Northrop, Bob Sweiringa, and Art Wyatt). Appreciation also goes to Jim Leisenring, former Director of the Research and Technical Activities Staff (and now a Board Member), who not only provided us with access to his people, office space, and other amenities during our visits, but also encouraged us to look at the FASB with an outsider's objective viewpoint. Special thanks go to J. T. Ball, Assistant Director of RTA, and Reed Storey, Senior Technical Advisor, for their hours of time reading our manuscript and answering questions about the Board and its predecessors. We also appreciate the time and attention we received from Paul Kolton (Chairman of the Financial Accounting Standards Advisory Committee), Paul Simpson (Executive Director of FASAC), Joe LaGambina (Executive Vice President of the Financial Accounting Foundation), and Bob Van Riper (Public Relations Counsel). We also appreciate the time and information we received from Project Managers Diana Kahn, Bob Wilkins (especially for his help with the Defeasance project), Joan Amble, and Halsey Bullen, and from Neal McGrath (Practice Fellow). Thanks for other assistance to Jack Lorenz (Human Resources Director) and his assistant Shirley O'Neill.

We also wish to thank those who reviewed materials for us: Dr. Ed Ketz at Pennsylvania State University (who was called on several times and responded very helpfully and quickly), Dr. Todd Johnson of the University of Houston at Clear Lake (a former FASB Project Manager), Dr. Robert Freeman of the University of Florida (another former Project Manager), Dr. Ed Swanson of Texas A&M (a former FASB Faculty Fellow), and Dr. Martin Gosman of Boston University.

We benefited greatly from the efforts of Dr. Paul Bahnson of the University of Colorado, a former graduate intern at the FASB.

Paul Miller
Rod Redding

CONTENTS

PROLOGUE

The Life Cycle of an Accounting Issue

July 7, 1982:

Exxon Completes Big Debt Restructuring, Raising 2nd-Quarter Profit $130 Million

BY DANIEL HERTZBERG
Staff Reporter of THE WALL STREET JOURNAL

NEW YORK—Exxon Corp. said it completed a massive debt restructuring that bolstered its balance sheet and added about $130 million to second-quarter earnings.

The transaction was the latest in a series of steps by the oil giant to shore up its sagging profit.

The restructuring allowed Exxon to remove from its balance sheet six long-term debt issues sold between 1967 and 1979, with a face value of $515 million. Exxon, however, took all of that debt off its books at a cost of only $312 million because the older bonds are selling far below face value.

For each issue, Exxon bought a portfolio of federal government and agency securities and placed them with a trustee; the cash generated by these securities is sufficient to meet interest and principal payments on each issue. This allowed Exxon to take the debt off its books without actually buying back the older issues.

The older Exxon bonds, which bear interest coupons of 5.8% to 6.7%, are selling at a sharp discount from their face value to match higher yields available on recently issued bonds. As a result, Exxon was able to buy for $312 million government securities needed for the "refunding."

The difference between this purchase cost and the $515 million face value of the bonds allowed Exxon to realize a $130 million after-tax gain in the second quarter, the company said.

In the first quarter, Exxon earned $1.24 billion, or $1.43 a share, down about 23% from the year earlier. Revenue in the 1982 quarter was $27.11 billion, down about 10%. Second-quarter results aren't yet available.

Exxon's earnings and cash flow have been hurt by the world oil surplus, which struck international oil companies such as Exxon particu-

larly hard because they are locked into buying relatively expensive crude oil from Saudi Arabia.

The debt changes are an attempt "to buoy up earnings and cash flow when they are still suffering from a margin squeeze and a strong dollar, which is hurting overseas refining and market profitability," said Sanford I. Margoshes, an oil analyst at Bache Halsey Stuart Shields & Co.

He said the move "should be viewed in the context of other efforts to maximize cash availability, including layoffs and deferrals of major capital-intensive projects such as synthetic fuels."

Exxon recently has used another financing tool, the debt-for-equity swap, to bolster its earnings and balance sheet. In these cases, a corporation exchanges newly issued shares of its stock for outstanding debt, usually older issues. Since last November, Exxon has completed three such swaps—retiring a total of $147 million of debt.

Allan Harrison, an Exxon assistant treasurer, said the refunding will be financed out of cash balances and, possibly, from short-term borrowings. He said that Exxon later may issue medium-term debt to finance the transaction.

The latest move, along with the earlier debt-for-equity swaps, practically eliminates parent Exxon Corp.'s long-term debt, which totaled $627 million last Dec. 31. However, long-term debt of Exxon Pipeline Co. and other Exxon subsidiaries totaled an additional $4.53 billion as of that date.

Last May, Exxon said it planned to raise as much as $500 million by selling debt securities this year. The external financing will be the first Exxon debt sold in the U.S. since 1976, and analysts viewed the announcement as another sign of financial pressure on the company.

August 9, 1982:

FASB Turns Thumbs Down on Taxable Defeasances

The *Financial Accounting Standards Board* last week effectively squelched the growing corporate enthusiasm (*CFW,* 7/5) for defeasances of taxable corporate debt. In an informal vote last Wednesday [August 4, 1982], five of the seven board members opposed a staff recommendation to allow corporations to use the same accounting treatment for "in-substance" defeasances of taxable debt as for defeasances of tax-exempt debt, said *Robert Wilkins,* FASB project manager.

Since it is the accounting treatment, not any substantial economic benefits, which has made in-substance defeasances so popular recently, say investment bankers and accountants (*CFW,* 7/26), any move by FASB to eliminate the accounting advantages of such deals would dramatically cut, if not entirely eliminate, their popularity. The accounting benefits stem from a corporation's ability, through a defeasance, to take debt off its books immediately while deferring the tax bite from the capital gain.

Adding to the near-unanimity—the two members not opposing the staff proposal nonetheless expressed reservations about in-substance defeasances, Wilkins said. Moreover, there were indications that the board intended its vote to be taken as a signal by the financial community. What's more, an SEC staffer said Friday [August 6, 1982] the commission staff is mulling a release warning corporations against using defeasance accounting for in-substance defeasances pending final FASB action.

Sources noted that last week's move does not in itself make any changes in permissible accounting practices on in-substance defeasances,

for which there are no rules right now. Indeed, formal changes require an exposure draft—expected late next month or in October—and public comment, and would likely not be made until January. But, said Wilkins, "accountants may have a reluctance to continue with [an] accounting treatment which they know will probably not be permitted next January." *Walter Schuetze,* partner, *Peat, Marwick, Mitchell* [and former FASB member], put it more bluntly: "The deals are probably squelched."

Certainly that was the opinion of most investment bankers who have been working on such deals. While there might conceivably be some way to get deals in under the wire, said *D. Barry O'Connor,* managing director, *Blyth, Eastman Paine Webber,* "my initial reaction is [that] without the accounting benefits most corporations wouldn't do the deals. It's bad news." Making it particularly galling for Blyth, he added, was the fact that the firm had lined up a $300 million defeasance deal with a major oil company which had just gone to its board with the deal when the news broke last week. "We were just waiting to hear from them," he said glumly, adding he expected the deal would now be cancelled. And an official at one...firm reportedly complained directly to the FASB. "We've poured tens of thousands of dollars into this effort," he wailed, "and now you've sent it all up in smoke." The one hope, sources noted, is that between now and January FASB might change its mind. That has happened, although rarely, they said, adding that a heavy lobbying effort would undoubtedly be launched.

SOURCE: *Corporate Financing Week,* a publication of Institutional Investor, August 9, 1982.

August 13, 1982:

Debt-Reduction Method Draws Concern of SEC

Staff Expected to Seek Halt to 'Defeasance,' Used By Exxon, Kellogg Co.

BY DANIEL HERTZBERG
Staff Reporter of THE WALL STREET JOURNAL

NEW YORK—An increasingly popular financing method that has enabled some major corporations to wipe long-term debt off their books and boost earnings has run into trouble with the Securities and Exchange Commission and accounting rules makers.

The technique, known as "defeasance," has enabled Exxon Corp. and some other U.S. companies to eliminate large chunks of debt from their balance sheets without actually having to buy back bonds they previously sold to investors.

The method is regarded with concern by some accountants and regulators, in part because it has allowed corporations such as Exxon to realize special earnings gains. Last month, Exxon said it was adding about $130 million to second quarter earnings through the practice.

However, the SEC staff is expected to ask the commission next week to declare a moratorium on the use of defeasance by U.S. companies, SEC officials said yesterday.

SEC officials said the proposed moratorium is intended to reinforce actions taken last week by the Financial Accounting Standards Board, the rule-making body of the accounting profession. The FASB tentatively concluded that corporations can't extinguish debt in this manner unless they were specifically authorized to do so under the terms of the original bonds.

News of the possible SEC action has already triggered a flurry of warnings by accounting firms to their corporate clients. A rule like that being discussed by the SEC staff would "seriously reduce the advantages" of defeasance transactions for U.S. corporations, warned John J. Fox, director of accounting and SEC consulting at the accounting firm of Coopers & Lybrand.

Sarah Fogg, an FASB project manager, says some accountants are concerned that "debt is being taken off the balance sheet when there really is an ongoing obligation." For example, she says, if a company files for bankruptcy, its bonds might become immediately due for payment. In this case, the securities deposited with the trustee mightn't be enough to pay off bond holders, yet the corporation's balance sheet wouldn't show any obligation.

Accountants said it isn't known if any SEC or FASB actions would affect past transactions like Exxon's.

An Exxon spokesman said, "We feel the action we took was in accordance with generally accepted accounting principles that now exist, and our auditors have agreed." He added that the FASB proposal isn't final and is subject "to much review and comment."

November 30, 1983:

FASB Adopts, 4-3, Controversial Method that Critics Assert Allows 'Instant' Profit

BY LEE BERTON

Staff Reporter of THE WALL STREET JOURNAL

NEW YORK—The Financial Accounting Standards Board approved a controversial accounting technique that critics say allows companies to create "instant" earnings.

The FASB, the rule-making body for the accounting profession, was itself sharply divided on the method, called "defeasance." It approved the rule by a 4-3 vote, with one of the negative votes being cast by Donald Kirk, FASB chairman. In August 1982, the Securities and Exchange Commission temporarily banned use of the technique, pending a ruling by the FASB.

Using "defeasance," companies can reduce debt on their balance sheets by creating a trust to service it. The device takes several forms, but in one variation a company buys government securities at a discount and places them in a trust, pledging the future income from the securities to pay off the interest and principal due on its own debt securities as they mature. The company scratches the debt from its balance sheet. Then, because the discounted government securities cost less than the potential cost of actually retiring the company's debt at face value, the company records a paper profit on its income statement.

Ruling Is Narrow

The FASB ruling permits defeasance only for a trust that purchases certain government or government-guaranteed securities at a discount. It doesn't include other types of transactions, such as selling the bonds to other companies rather than setting up a trust with government securities.

While the SEC is expected to lift its ban within a week or so, some commissioners still have reservations about defeasance. "I'm queasy about it because the debt is still legally debt, and the creation of earnings appears to be a charade," says John Evans, an SEC commissioner retiring on Friday.

Prior to the SEC's moratorium last year, a slew of companies, including Exxon Corp., New York, and Kellogg Co., Battle Creek, Mich., used defeasance.

Two Cases Cited

Steven P. Johnson, an FASB project manager, said that under the new rule, Exxon would have been permitted to retire its debt while Kellogg wouldn't.

Last year, Exxon placed in trust six bond issues totaling $515 million; the trust purchased $313 million in government securities to service the bonds. The government securities generated sufficient interest to pay the principal and interest outstanding on the bonds. As a result, Exxon gained $132 million in profits for its 1982 second quarter.

Kellogg, on the other hand, sold $75 million in $8\frac{5}{8}\%$ notes, due Oct. 1, 1985, to several "industrial companies" for more than $64 million, increasing its 1982 second-quarter earnings $5.7 million after taxes, according to Lou R. Somers, Kellogg's vice president, finance.

A. Clarence Sampson, the SEC's chief accountant, said that both Exxon and Kellogg would be permitted to retain their defeasance transactions because no accounting rules on the technique existed last year. "The SEC issued the moratorium because it felt that corporations shouldn't be permitted to create accounting rules before such rules exist," he added.

December 5, 1983:

De- or Misfeasance?

A Look at the New FASB Ruling

BY ROMAN L. WEIL, University of Chicago

It's the season for window dressing, and even the Financial Accounting Standards Board is getting in on the act. It has just presented corporate managers with the opportunity to boost reported income, lower the debt-equity ratio and (in some cases) increase their own compensation. But if a corporation seizes the apparently attractive opportunity, its shareholders will likely suffer.

The FASB's year-end gift to corporate types is its new accounting standard (Statement of Financial Accounting Standards No. 76, November 1983) on "de facto defeasances."

Before the new FASB ruling, the gain from a decline in the market value of a liability would appear in income only when the firm repurchased and retired the debt.

Many bondholders just don't want to sell their bonds before maturity, perhaps because they are reluctant to report the realized loss that accounting rules require if they sell their bonds. So corporate financial managers have found a way to achieve the economic equivalent of retiring all the bonds before their maturity without having to engage in costly repurchase transactions and without imposing realized accounting losses on the bondholders.

Borrower Co., for example, can purchase U.S. government securities with cash throw-offs (interest and principal repayments) equal to those required to service its own bond issue. Then Borrower Co. turns over the just-acquired Treasuries to an independent trustee, along with the obligation to make debt-service payments on the outstanding Borrower Co. bond issue. In substance, Borrower Co. has retired the bonds. The FASB's new standard simply requires that this transaction, called a "de facto defeasance," be treated on the books as though it were a formal debt retirement, and that, in my opinion, is quite proper.

What's wrong is that under the FASB rule, a borrower can report a gain only by eliminating *all* risk of default from the bondholders' viewpoint: The borrower must use government bonds

to defease its own bonds. In effect, the bondholders trade risky corporate bonds for "riskless" government bonds with exactly the same cash throw-offs. The shareholders pay the premium needed to reduce the bondholders' risk. Less-risky debt is always more costly than riskier debt with the same promised cash flows. And the difference in cost increases with both the risk and the life of the bond.

Who does benefit? The bondholders will find their securities more valuable—the market price of the outstanding bond issue will rise at the time of defeasance and thereafter should track the market price of the government issue used to replace it. The trust company that will clip and collect the government bond coupons, then send payments to the current bondholders, will earn fees. Management, whose compensation contracts contain bonus clauses based on reported income, may earn extra wages. Finally, scholars will have a rare opportunity to study the reactions of the financial markets to an event with (favorable) accounting implications different from the (unfavorable) cash-flow implications and economic substance of the transaction.

Who loses? The common shareholders. But it will take academic accountants a year or two to document the wealth loss to shareholders of companies who engage in de facto defeasance transactions to voluntarily retire debt.

Certainly, there can be times when a company's management decides it's good financial policy to retire debt. And defeasance may be preferred to outright repurchase for tax reasons, particularly if the issuing firm has such a good credit rating that the defeasance premium is low. But, if management must borrow new funds in order to make the swap, or if mere window dressing of the financial statements appears to be the motive, beware. After all, why would management think it worthwhile to transfer wealth from its shareholders to its bondholders merely to report higher accounting income? ∎

The preceding articles from the business press have been presented here in order to illustrate a number of important points about the process for setting financial accounting standards in the United States. In particular, the reader should note the following:

- A new and unusual type of financial transaction occurred—the "in-substance defeasance" of debt. It was developed and used by several large corporations in order to improve their apparent (and possibly actual) financial position.

- A controversial question (an "issue") arose in the business community concerning the method that would best reflect the results of the new transaction in the financial statements.

- Different groups within the business community preferred different answers to the question—some wanted to recognize a gain on the income statement and remove the debt from the statement of financial position, while others did not think that either step should be taken.

- The groups involved in the debate over the issue included the management of corporations, investment analysts, investment bankers, investors, creditors, independent auditors, and government regulators.

- The groups tended to agree that the issue needed to be resolved by the issuance of authoritative guidance in order that uniform practice would be established.

- The groups did not look to a government agency for the resolution of the issue but to a nongovernmental organization called the **Financial Accounting Standards Board** (the FASB), in Stamford, Connecticut, which is located 40 miles from New York City.

- Although the federal Securities and Exchange Commission (the SEC) did act to establish a "moratorium" on using the disputed procedures to account for defeasances, the step was only temporary, pending the development of the FASB's authoritative position.

- The process for resolving the issue involved a number of steps, beginning with the creation of the project on the FASB's agenda, continuing with much discussion, and culminating with the issuance of the final Statement of Financial Accounting Standards. The elapsed time between the FASB's initial meeting and the issuance of the Statement was approximately 15 months.

- The various groups that were to be affected by the proposed accounting attempted to shape the standard. Particular attention should be addressed to the comment in the *Corporate Financing Week* article that a "heavy lobbying effort would undoubtedly be launched."

- In the view of at least one observer (the author of the *Barron's* article), a defeasance does not produce benefits for the stockholders of the corporation but does benefit bondholders, management, and investment bankers.

- Everyone involved in the debate seemed to think that the numbers reported in the financial statements actually make a difference. Of course, this fact does not prove that financial accounting numbers actually affect decisions, but it does show that the information in the financial statements is thought to be important. Because the numbers are thought to be important, it follows that issues concerning them are also important.
- The reporters for the business press called on people from many different occupations for their views on the issue. Quotations were provided from comments made by an SEC official, independent auditors, corporate representatives, investment bankers, stockbrokers, and accounting professors. Also notice the references to comments made by FASB **project managers** and the fact that no comments were made by the Board Members themselves.

1

Financial Accounting
and the FASB

The primary goal of this book is to provide its readers with knowledge about the Financial Accounting Standards Board—its **people**, its **processes**, and the **politics** of standards setting. This knowledge will help them understand more about an important part of the accounting profession, and thereby help prepare them for more successful careers, whether they have chosen to be accountants or to be involved with the business community in some other capacity.

By the time that this book is studied, the reader should be able to describe:

☐ The reasons for having a formal standards-setting process.
☐ The groups involved in the process.
☐ The methods used to set standards.
☐ How the FASB's processes are affected by such political practices as persuasion, negotiation, compromise, and consensus development.
☐ Some of the controversial issues that the FASB has attempted to resolve.
☐ The FASB's Conceptual Framework project.
☐ The prospects for the future of the FASB.

Furthermore, the reader should have a grasp of the history of standards setting as well as the current activities of the FASB.

This first chapter provides the basic foundation for much that is developed more completely in the rest of the book. In doing so, it answers the following questions:

- What is financial accounting, and why is it considered to be important?
- Who are the groups most interested in financial accounting, and what is the nature of their interest?
- Why should differences among these groups be resolved?
- What is the basic structure of the FASB?
- From where does the FASB derive its authority?
- What procedures does the FASB follow in setting standards?
- Is the FASB a political institution?

WHAT IS FINANCIAL ACCOUNTING, AND WHY IS IT CONSIDERED TO BE IMPORTANT?

As a brief definition, financial accounting is the practice of providing financial information about an economic entity to people who are not actively engaged in its management. Thus, it does not include management accounting, which is concerned with providing information to those who *are* actively engaged in managing the entity. Nor does it include regulatory accounting whereby entities in regulated industries (such as utilities, communications media, and financial institutions) provide financial and other types of information to governmental bodies charged with protecting the public interest. Finally, it does not include the reporting of information to taxing authorities, such as the Internal Revenue Service.

Financial accounting is considered important because of the role it plays in the operation of the U.S. economy. The links in the relationship between financial accounting and the efficient operation of the economy are represented schematically in Exhibit 1–1.

The Relationship between the Economy and Financial Accounting

In simple terms, the economy can be viewed as a means for generating wealth, which in turn provides for the necessities and amenities of life. The economy is also the means by which society accomplishes other goals, such as social stability, full employment, and improvement in the standard of living. Consequently, the efficient functioning of the economy is important for the standard of living of the United States and the world.

In order for the economy to operate, it must have **productive resources**, or goods that are used to provide more goods and services. These resources include such things as machinery, buildings, and inventory. For every dollar of output produced in the economy, more dollars are invested in productive resources. In order to support a gross national product of about $4 trillion, many more trillions of dollars must be available.

EXHIBIT 1–1   Why Is Financial Accounting Important?

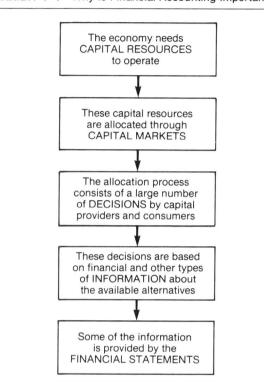

Where, then, do these resources come from? Many of them are purchased by entities (corporations) with wealth that they generate through their own profitable activities. In contrast to this **internal** source, many other resources are purchased with funds that are raised **externally**; that is, the funds are obtained through investments by owners (stockholders) or through loans from nonowners (creditors). The mutual satisfaction of the needs of stockholders and creditors and the needs of corporations takes place through **capital markets**. In a broad sense, these markets encompass all transactions between capital providers and consumers. Thus, they include not only organized marketplaces (such as stock exchanges or options markets) but also private situations, such as transactions between individual borrowers and bankers.

The purpose of the capital markets is to allocate the available resources among those who want them. The mechanism of the allocation is the price of the resources, which takes the form of expected returns to investors and creditors. That is, they will invest or loan their wealth only when they believe that they will receive an adequate profit (in the form of dividends, interest, and appreciation) in light of the risks they face. Likewise, corporations will acquire resources only when the cost of capital that they face is appropriate for the circumstances.

Essentially, the capital markets allow many people and institutions to come together to do business. Alternative funding sources are considered by corporations, alternative investments are considered by stockholders and creditors, decisions are reached, and contracts are entered into. For example, corporations obtain resources by issuing stock, and thereby create new ownership rights. They also issue bonds in return for borrowed resources, and thereby create new creditors' rights. Additional borrowing takes place through leases and loans. Furthermore, the capital markets encompass transactions strictly between investors and creditors with no participation by a corporation. (For example, stocks and bonds are traded between individuals.) These transactions are important because they involve many buyers and sellers and thus allow the market forces to work more effectively.

Thus, many, many **decisions** are reached in the capital markets, and the process of making them involves assessments of future events. In particular, risks and returns are assessed and prices are established through competition. Although there are many other factors to consider, the decisions are generally financial in nature, in the sense that they involve money.

The lifeblood of all rational decision making is **information**, which has the basic purpose of reducing uncertainty about predictions of future events and conditions. In order to act rationally, providers of capital need information about the alternative uses of their resources. Similarly, rational consumers of capital (or their advisers) need to know about the costs associated with the available alternative sources of funds.

Although many different types of information come into play in making these decisions, **financial information** is especially important because it is expressed in terms of money, which serves as a common denominator for allowing different investment and credit opportunities to be compared.

One major source of some (but certainly not all or even most) of this financial information is the **financial statements** prepared and distributed by corporations, usually as part of a more encompassing financial report.[1] **Financial accounting** is the process by which these statements are prepared.

Types of financial information. There are many different types of financial information. Some of it is concerned with the future (such as forecasts), while some of it is historical in nature (such as financial statements). Some of it is general to the economy or broad sectors of it (such as reports on interest rates or market sizes), while some of it is specific to a particular entity (such as financial statements). Furthermore, some of the

---

[1] A complete set of financial statements includes (1) the statement of financial position (balance sheet), (2) the income statement, (3) the statement of cash flows (formerly the statement of changes in financial position), and (4) the statement of stockholders' equity.

information is prepared by or on behalf of certain investors and creditors for their own benefit (such as recommendations from financial analysts or bond rating agencies like Moody's), while some of it is provided directly by corporations for distribution to all investors, creditors, and others (such as financial statements).

Summary. Financial accounting is considered to be important to the economy as a whole because it provides information that can be used in the capital markets to help investors and creditors make decisions that affect the allocation of capital resources among the participants in economic activity. If these decisions are made in the light of useful financial information, it is more likely that the economy will be more efficient. And, if the economy is more efficient, it is more likely that society's goals will be fulfilled.

Another View on the Importance of Financial Accounting

From a different perspective, financial accounting is important to many people because their personal standards of living depend on their knowledge of its practices. These people include independent auditors who review financial statements for their propriety, private accountants who prepare financial statements describing their employer corporations, and financial analysts who use them to develop recommendations for their clients. Financial accounting can also be important to managers of corporations because their job security, compensation, status, power, and other aspects of their self-esteem may very well be affected by the picture of their performance provided in the financial statements.[2] An awareness of these behavioral factors is very helpful for comprehending the processes used for setting standards.

WHO ARE THE GROUPS MOST INTERESTED IN FINANCIAL ACCOUNTING, AND WHAT IS THE NATURE OF THEIR INTEREST?

The news stories in the Prologue and the preceding pages have touched briefly on several groups of people who are interested in financial accounting.

---

[2]The importance of these effects is suggested by the views expressed by Dr. Roman Weil's article from *Barron's,* presented in the Prologue. The general idea that accounting policy decisions are shaped by these sorts of factors is the basis for the "positive" theory of accounting. For more information, the following should be consulted: Dale Gerboth, "Research, Intuition, and Politics in Accounting Inquiry," *The Accounting Review,* July 1973, pp. 475–82; Charles Horngren, "The Marketing of Accounting Standards," *Journal of Accountancy,* October 1973, pp. 61–66; Ross Watts and Jerold Zimmerman, "Toward a Positive Theory of Determination of Accounting Standards," *The Accounting Review,* January 1978, pp. 112–34; Ross Watts and Jerold Zimmerman, "The Demand for and Supply of Accounting Theories: The Market for Excuses," *The Accounting Review,* April 1979, pp. 273–305; and Ross Watts and Jerold Zimmerman, *Positive Accounting Theory* (Englewood Cliffs, N.J.: Prentice-Hall, 1986).

This section examines them more closely and shows how they often have competing interests in the reporting process.

As demonstrated by their participation in the deliberations on the defeasance issues, certain **government regulators** are interested because they are charged with the responsibility of protecting the capital markets from inefficiencies in allocating capital resources, including those created by the publication of false or otherwise misleading information. The Securities and Exchange Commission (SEC) has this specific responsibility. Other regulators (such as the Interstate Commerce Commission and the Federal Energy Regulatory Commission) occasionally participate in the financial accounting standards-setting process when their reporting requirements coincide with the practices used in reporting to investors and creditors. Their participation in standards setting is quite appropriate because of the role they are supposed to fill. Their goal in participating is often to encourage the disclosure of more information to financial statement users.

Providers of capital resources are naturally quite interested because they may be able to affect their risks and expected returns by using financial accounting information. This group of **financial statement users** includes actual and potential investors and lenders. It also includes financial analysts (both independent practitioners and those employed by brokerage firms) who advise resource providers on the suitability of various alternative investments. They participate in the standards-setting process in order to increase the likelihood that they (or their clients) will receive at least a fair price for their resources. Consequently, their goal in the process is often to increase the amount of information disclosed. On the other hand, certain users of financial statements have access to private sources of information that they have been able to use to increase their wealth; it is only reasonable to expect them to want to *limit* the amount of information provided in the statements.

Managers of corporations are interested in financial accounting because their companies' access to resources (and the prices of those resources) can be affected by financial accounting information. As mentioned, if the managers' own compensation (or other aspects of their well-being) might be affected by financial accounting information, they are especially interested in the message conveyed in the financial statements. Consequently, they participate in the standards-setting process in order to have more control over a significant part of their surroundings. In general, they are more in control when there are fewer requirements for the type and quantity of information to be presented in the financial statements.

Independent auditors are interested in financial accounting and standards setting because of their special role in auditing information reported to investors and creditors by companies. Specifically, their task is to add credibility to the information reported by management in the financial statements by performing an audit of the financial statements and attaching an "opinion" to them. Because their professional reputations and livelihoods depend on the perceived quality of their audits, auditors face the risk of a potentially high penalty for failure. Consequently, their participation in the standards-setting process often is directed toward producing more auditable information. This tendency for auditors to protect their self-interest is often balanced by a strong sense of concern for the public interest, which is usually more closely aligned with statement users' needs or the efficiency of the capital markets' allocations of resources.

Additionally, as shown in the news stories in the Prologue, auditors are often consulted as independent experts on difficult issues. Their view is considered useful because of their apparent detachment from the problem in contrast to the bias that statement users and statement providers may have or appear to have.

Instructors of accounting constitute another group involved in financial accounting. They are interested in the standards-setting process because they commit their careers to understanding accounting and to helping others understand it. Of all the groups participating in the standards-setting process, they are generally perceived as being the most independent and objective because of their social role as educators and because they are not financially involved like the others. However, the political nature of the standards-setting process tends to limit the effectiveness of this group because its members have less power than the other participants.

In summary, a variety of groups are interested in financial accounting. They have different points of view and interests, even to the extent of having goals for the standards-setting process that are in direct or nearly direct opposition. Furthermore, they each have power and influence and attempt to affect the process in ways that protect or advance their interests. The next section deals with the question of why it is considered desirable to attempt to resolve their differences on financial accounting issues.

WHY SHOULD DIFFERENCES AMONG THESE GROUPS BE RESOLVED?

A fundamental premise underlying current financial accounting standards setting is that **uniformity** in the practices used by all reporting companies is generally preferable to diversity. The origins of this premise lie in the view that valid, and thus useful, comparisons among alternative investments can be made only if the financial information is **comparable**. As explanation, comparability exists when like events and conditions are described similarly and when unlike events and conditions are described differently. If significant real economic similarities or differences exist but are not revealed in the accounting reports, it is argued, then users of those reports will not make efficient allocation decisions.[3]

---

[3]It should be noted that uniformity is not sufficient to produce comparability. For example, no manufacturing company recognizes an asset for its human resources; even though all manufacturers follow this uniform practice, their financial statements do not provide comparable information because the employees of all companies do not have the same economic value and because probably none of them have the zero value reflected on the statement of financial position. For a more complete discussion of these points, see Statement of Financial Accounting Concepts No. 2 (paragraphs 111–119), issued by the FASB in 1978.

From a more behavioral perspective, uniformity is generally considered desirable because it helps protect financial statement users against managers' natural bias to prepare their "scorecards" so that their performance looks better than it may really be. If managers are constrained in their choices, it is argued, they are less able to provide biased information and better decisions are more likely to be made.

On the other hand, uniformity helps protect corporate management against less scrupulous managers of other corporations who might attempt to gain an advantage in the capital markets by providing deliberately misleading information. Furthermore, by following an authoritative external rule, management may be protected against after-the-fact allegations from unsuccessful investors that the company's financial statements made its securities appear to be a better investment than they really were.

Uniformity also protects auditors because the rules provide an external basis for their judgments. Specifically, a conclusion that the financial statements were prepared in compliance with a published set of standards is more easily reached (and far more defensible) than a conclusion that the statements disclose the "truth" about the company. In attesting to compliance, the auditor's decisions are relatively objective and supportable with hard evidence. In reaching a judgment about "truth," the outcome would tend to be more conjecture than fact, and the auditor would be exposed to a high risk of failure and demands for retribution by those who relied on the audit opinion.

Because of these considerations, there appears to be general agreement that most participants (and the economy as a whole) are better off with the regulation of the flow of information from corporations to investors and creditors as accomplished by the establishment of a uniform set of accounting standards. The term *generally accepted accounting principles* (or **GAAP**) is the name given to the set of agreed-upon rules and guidelines. As will be made clear later in this book, not everyone agrees that standards are needed or that they are cost effective.

Because different views exist on the question of what rule should be created to deal with a given situation (as seen for defeasances in the Prologue), it follows that there must be some process for resolving the differences. That mechanism is presently located in the **Financial Accounting Standards Board**. In general terms, the FASB's role is to resolve issues concerning the usefulness of various types of financial information in particular circumstances. In performing this task, the FASB must gather and sift evidence about that usefulness while taking into consideration the interests of the various parties affected by its standards. The output of its process becomes part of GAAP.

The next three sections of this chapter deal briefly with the FASB's structure, the source of its authority, and its procedures. Subsequent chapters provide more detailed information.

EXHIBIT 1–2   The Structure of the FASB

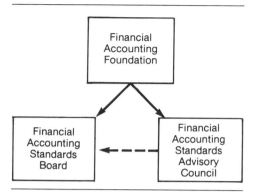

WHAT IS THE BASIC STRUCTURE OF THE FASB?

The Financial Accounting Standards Board is the operating arm of a three-part organizational structure represented in Exhibit 1–2.

The **Financial Accounting Foundation** is the parent organization, and its trustees constitute the governing body. The Foundation is recognized as a nonprofit organization under the Internal Revenue Code. The Foundation has an Executive Director and is administered by its 16 trustees. The two primary tasks of the trustees are to raise funds for the operation of the organization and to appoint members to the FASB.[4] Under the Foundation's bylaws, the trustees are not to interfere in any way with the standards-setting work of the FASB. Of course, their power to appoint and reappoint members assures that they do have indirect influence over the process in the long run just as the president of the United States can influence future decisions of the Supreme Court through his appointments of the justices.

The **Financial Accounting Standards Advisory Council** (FASAC) is a group of approximately 30 influential persons. The number actually serving on FASAC varies from year to year; the bylaws merely call for at least 20 members to be appointed. The actual number serving has grown larger to obtain representation of more groups of interested parties. The purpose of the Council is to advise the FASB, particularly on the issues that exist in financial accounting and on the priorities that should be placed on resolving them. FASAC also advises the FASB on the suitability of its tentative resolutions of

---

[4]The trustees also raise funds for and appoint the members of the Governmental Accounting Standards Board (GASB), which develops standards to be used in preparing financial statements for state and local governmental entities.

the issues that the Board is addressing. The members of the Council are appointed by the trustees of the Foundation.

FROM WHERE DOES THE FASB DERIVE ITS AUTHORITY?

From the articles in the Prologue, it is clear that the Financial Accounting Standards Board has authority for setting standards; because of this authority, some people mistakenly assume that the FASB is actually a government agency.[5] The previous discussion has shown that it is a privately funded, nongovernmental entity. Nonetheless, the FASB's authority does depend largely on its endorsement by governmental bodies, particularly the federal Securities and Exchange Commission (SEC) and state-level regulatory agencies. It derives additional authority from other nongovernmental sources. The relationships between these organizations and the FASB are illustrated in Exhibit 1–3. In particular, the reader should note how the different organiza tions can be seen to represent the interests of the various constituent groups.

The Securities and Exchange Commission

In its founding legislation (passed in 1933 and 1934), the **Securities and Exchange Commission** was given authority to establish accounting principles for its **registrants**, which is the name given to those corporations that must comply with its reporting requirements. These companies must meet certain size tests and have owners in more than one state. Normally, a company must comply with the SEC's registration requirements if it has at least $5 million in assets and/or 500 stockholders. Such companies must register their securities (stocks and bonds) before they are issued to the public and must subsequently file regular periodic and special reports with the SEC. The Commission's statutory authority over its registrants can be represented as illustrated below:

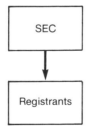

The early Commissioners of the SEC decided against developing a new set of accounting standards to be used by registrants; instead, they adopted the

---

[5]Some think the "F" in FASB stands for "Federal."

EXHIBIT 1–3 The Sources of the FASB's Authority

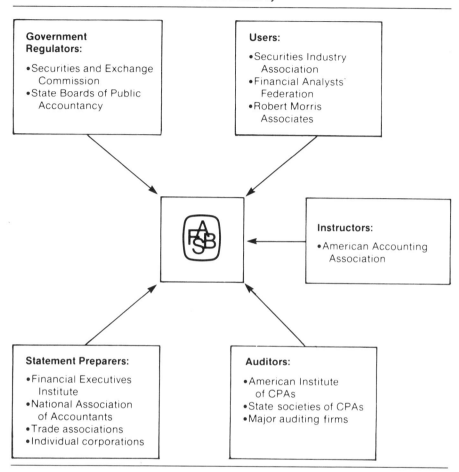

strategy of relying on existing principles for which there was "substantial authoritative support." This policy was established in 1938 in the SEC's Accounting Series Release No. 4. In effect, this action shifted the authority for rule making to the **American Institute of Accountants** (now the **American Institute of Certified Public Accountants**, or AICPA), which shortly thereafter formed the **Committee on Accounting Procedure** to resolve controversial issues. The committee was succeeded in 1959 by the AICPA's **Accounting Principles Board**. Both of these organizations are described in the appendix to Chapter 2.

Then, largely because giving authority to a committee composed primarily of independent auditors did not appear to provide an equal opportunity for all interested groups to participate in (and to affect the outcome of) the standards-setting process, the FASB was formed in 1973. In the same year, the SEC specifically recognized the Board as the official source of generally accepted accounting principles. The following endorsement was first published in Accounting Series Release No. 150 and was incorporated into the SEC's Financial Reporting Release No. 1 in 1982:

> ...the Commission intends to continue its policy of looking to the private sector for leadership in establishing and improving accounting principles and standards.... [Consequently,] principles, standards and practices promulgated by the FASB in its Statements and Interpretations will be considered by the Commission as having substantial authoritative support, and those contrary to such FASB promulgations will be considered to have no such support.

Thus, this diagram is more descriptive of the relationship among the SEC, the FASB, and the SEC's registrants:

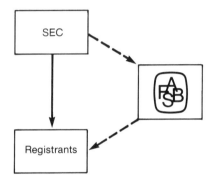

The dotted line represents the fact that the FASB has authority only for the setting of accounting principles—the SEC remains the sole authority for regulating other aspects of corporate governance, such as the solicitation of stockholder proxies and the trading of securities by so-called insiders, who include managers and major stockholders. It must be emphasized that the FASB has not been delegated any enforcement authority by the SEC. Furthermore, the FASB has only limited authority for establishing accounting principles because the SEC can adopt its own rules where the FASB is silent or when the Commission thinks that other practices will provide more useful information. These powers of the Commission have rarely been exercised. Notable situations in which they have been used include the SEC's decision in 1978 to reject the FASB's answer to the question of how oil and gas producing companies should measure their income and the FASB's issuance of Statement of Financial Accounting Standards No. 33 in 1979 requiring the presentation of supplemental information about the effects of changing prices.

In addition, as shown in the articles in the Prologue, the SEC can act to encourage the FASB to undertake the resolution of an issue. Typically, overt pressure from the Commission is not apparent; rather, the SEC and the FASB operate within an atmosphere of "mutual nonsurprise."[6]

State Regulatory Authorities

Another governmental source of authority for the FASB is the endorsement of its pronouncements by state-level agencies that license public accountants. The task of these agencies (usually called **State Boards of Public Accountancy**) is to control certified public accountants' professional activities, primarily through two channels. A State Board is authorized first to identify sources of GAAP for auditors practicing under its jurisdiction, and second to establish means of enforcing compliance with GAAP. Usually through some type of ethics regulations, the FASB is recognized as the authority for establishing GAAP, but the enforcement authority is retained by the State Board.[7]

Additional credibility is given to the FASB by state authorities through their use of the **Uniform CPA Examination** in their licensing process. Because this exam (which is compiled by the AICPA) includes a large number of questions related to FASB pronouncements, the state authorities are essentially establishing the fact that a competent public accountant must have a thorough knowledge of FASB matters.

Nongovernmental Bodies

Nongovernmental support has also proven to be vital in establishing the authority of the FASB. For example, in May 1973, the AICPA endorsed FASB standards in its ethics rules for its members. Essentially, Rule 203 of the Institute's Code of Professional Ethics does not allow an auditor to state that a client's financial statements are prepared in accordance with GAAP when they do not comply with applicable FASB pronouncements. Rule 203 does allow an exception for circumstances in which compliance with GAAP will produce misleading information if the exception is clearly and completely described in the auditor's opinion. In practice, this exception is virtually never invoked. Because the Institute has no governmental authority, its strongest sanction for unethical behavior is merely to expel a CPA from its membership. However, this action can diminish the individual's reputation

---

[6]This expression was used in testimony by former FASB Chairman Don Kirk before the Subcommittee on Oversight and Investigations, Committee on Energy and Commerce, U.S. House of Representatives, February 20, 1985. Mr. Kirk attributes its first use to Dr. John C. Burton, who was the SEC's Chief Accountant from 1972 to 1976.

[7]This arrangement also requires the application of FASB rules to the financial statements of companies that are *not* SEC registrants. Because the FASB must shape its requirements to meet the needs of the SEC, complaints often arise that the FASB is not sensitive to the needs of smaller companies. This so-called standards overload problem is discussed in the Epilogue.

and ability to practice and can motivate AICPA members to comply with GAAP developed by the FASB.

The same effect is accomplished for members of **state professional societies** of CPAs that adopt an ethics rule similar to the AICPA's Rule 203. These societies are voluntary associations separate from the State Boards that grant licenses. Those CPAs who join a society are seeking some additional benefits, such as continuing education programs and access to life and disability insurance. The societies have their own ethics rules that usually correspond to those of the AICPA and that may or may not be different from the regulations established by the State Boards.

Other nongovernmental organizations have increased the **influence** of the FASB without adding to its authority in the same way as the SEC, the State Boards, and the AICPA. These other organizations' primary means of support for FASB is their participation in the standards-setting process. The most significant national organizations of this kind (and the typical orientation of their members) are:

- ☐ **Securities Industry Association** (SIA)
  —investment bankers
- ☐ **Financial Analysts Federation** (FAF)
  —investment advisers
- ☐ **Financial Executives Institute** (FEI)
  —corporate accounting officers at highest levels
- ☐ **National Association of Accountants** (NAA)
  —corporate accountants at all levels
- ☐ **American Accounting Association** (AAA)
  —accountants from various fields, but predominantly professors

Additional credibility has been attributed to FASB pronouncements through extensive participation in the Board's due process activities by individuals, corporations, trade associations, and public accounting firms. Together with the AICPA, these groups comprise six of the eight **sponsoring organizations** that have special powers in the governance of the Financial Accounting Foundation.[8]

Additional credibility is attributed to FASB pronouncements through extensive participation in the Board's due process activities by individuals, corporations, trade associations, and public accounting firms. One particularly active users' group is Robert Morris Associates, which is composed of bank lending officers. Examples of trade associations that have participated are the American Petroleum Institute and the Edison Electric Institute.

The complexity of the Board's position should be clear from this discussion. Specifically, it derives its real legal authority from its endorsement by

---

[8]The other two sponsoring organizations are the Government Finance Officers Association and the National Association of State Auditors, Comptrollers and Treasurers.

governmental bodies but depends on nongovernmental bodies for its funding and its governance. This arrangement inevitably produces ambiguities and controversy. Some aspects of these issues are discussed in the Epilogue.

WHAT PROCEDURES DOES THE FASB FOLLOW IN SETTING STANDARDS?

To accomplish its duties, the FASB must mobilize members of the business community[9] to participate in its procedures. Through their participation, the FASB is more capable of (1) identifying unresolved financial accounting questions, (2) ranking those questions in importance, (3) identifying the alternative answers, and (4) evaluating the answers to find the most suitable one for the present circumstances. Furthermore, by involving the community in extensive and thorough **due process procedures**, the Board can develop a more broadly based consensus in support of its conclusions than it could if it operated in a vacuum. The detailed steps in the due process are described in Chapter 3.

In going about its work, the FASB must focus on controversial issues. In the words of former Board Chairman Don Kirk,

> There are no easy, universally popular answers to most of the questions facing the FASB. Problems that are amenable to clear-cut solutions never reach the Board. The problems it is asked to deal with generally are those on which reasonable and informed people differ.[10]

Although the Board listens to the business community in identifying which issues to try to resolve, its members determine which projects are admitted to its agenda. However, they are closely advised on this point by FASAC and are not likely to be able to duck an issue because it promises to be difficult to resolve. The actual steps by which a project is created are also discussed in Chapter 3.

Chapter 4 describes a series of controversial issues that the FASB, its predecessors, and the accounting profession have faced over a number of years. As Don Kirk suggested, without controversy there is no need for the FASB, but with controversy there is need for debate and change. As a consequence, members of the profession need to be prepared to cope with changes in practice. In order to deal with such changes, it is helpful to understand the nature of the changes that have occurred in the past.

---

[9]In an unpublished report forwarded to the trustees of the Financial Accounting Foundation in 1985, a committee of the Financial Executives Institute identified the financial preparer constituency of the FASB as the "business community." The authors believe that this extremely narrow usage of the phrase is inappropriate because auditors, users, regulators, academicians, and the FASB are all part of the business community. Consequently, the phrase is used in this book in the more well-established sense to mean all who participate in business activity, rather than just corporate management.

[10]Testimony before the Subcommittee on Oversight and Investigations, Committee on Energy and Commerce. U.S. House of Representatives, February 20, 1985.

The Conceptual Framework

When a standards-setting body like the FASB faces controversial issues, particularly in a public arena, it is understandable that its members would want to deal with the questions one at a time rather than as parts of a larger whole. If a one-at-a-time (or ad hoc) approach is adopted, compromises and resolutions tend to take on customized forms to deal with the needs of specific constituents. Because different groups are affected differently by different issues, the standards setters can drift into this ad hoc approach under which each issue is resolved without regard to previously developed resolutions of others. For example, similar transactions may occur in two different industry settings and create what appear to be two separate problems, with the result that the standards setters would have to deal with two different constituent groups. If the ad hoc approach were to be used, the standards setters could compromise and reach a different consensus solution for the seemingly different problems. A similar result could occur if several years intervene between two projects and new appointees are serving on the authoritative body. These situations are generally considered to be undesirable because they may introduce inconsistencies and contradictions among standards that can rob the financial statements of comparability and other attributes of usefulness.

The ad hoc approach is also undesirable because it tends to create redundancy in discussions when the same basic issues are debated over and over again with the different constituents involved in different specific projects. For example, the Board and the affected constituents could come to an agreement as to the meaning of the term *asset* in the discussion of an issue in the utilities industry. Then, when a problem arose in the software industry and different people were involved in the deliberations, it would be necessary to debate once again what *asset* means.

To help avoid these problems, the FASB undertook the development of its own **Conceptual Framework** that attempts to establish a more global view of accounting and defines a number of basic terms. As the result of a number of practical considerations, the nature of the FASB and its processes do not allow these types of problems to be eliminated or avoided.

Because the Framework is important for understanding how the FASB works, Chapter 5 explains its fundamental components and the difficulties that the FASB faced in building it and continues to face in using it.

IS THE FASB A POLITICAL INSTITUTION?

The answer to the question of whether the FASB is a political institution depends, of course, on the definition of the term *political* that one chooses to adopt. There are two common definitions that need to be distinguished before going on to the answer. One holds that the term *political* (or *politics*) merely refers to the processes of **governing** an entity or activity. The second definition includes a connotation of **manipulation** of that system for the purpose of promoting one's self-interest to the detriment of others.

In applying the first definition, it can be seen that the FASB and any other organization (such as a company, a school, a church, a club, or even a family) is indeed political. In carrying out its tasks, the Board will inevitably make decisions that benefit some more than they benefit others. If it were possible for all participants to be better off as a result of an accounting standard, there would be no need for the standard because there would be no controversy. In all likelihood, everyone would be using the practice without having to be told to do so.

In making those decisions, it is equally inevitable that compromises among the constituents will be made in order to develop the necessary consensus to establish the standard as "generally accepted." A compromise may involve accepting less than the full amount of information that a particular group might like to see presented, or it may involve one party getting what it wants on one project in exchange for giving up what it wanted on another. While the process of reaching the compromise is inevitably political, there is no necessity that the process must involve any of the unsavory practices that are often connoted by the term *politics*.

However, as indicated by the reference to "lobbying" in one of the articles in the Prologue, it is readily apparent that many of the constituents in the Board's processes act out of **self-interest.** Indeed, it is the opportunity to seek favorable solutions from the Board that brings such great vitality and thoroughness to the standards-setting process.

For those who would disparage the presence of *any* politics in standards setting, it may be instructive to consider what alternative system could be implemented. In lieu of a deliberative body, a single "emperor" of accounting might be appointed to derive solutions from the logical analysis of a few basic fundamental "truths." However appealing that system might be, it is too simplistic because unambiguous principles have not yet been uncovered. Furthermore, it is inevitable that the emperor would impose some costs on some parties in excess of their benefits. In the same sense that taxation without representation is inherently unfair, something is lacking in a standards-setting system that does not call for participation by those affected by the standards.

The FASB's structure is designed to capture some of the advantages of both the participative and the "emperor" approaches. The due process procedures are established in order to give everyone an opportunity to protect their interests; however, the issues are not resolved by counting the votes of all those who participate. Rather, the Board Members have the powers of a collective emperor in the sense that they are given the authority to choose the final answer. But they are constrained by the need to obtain continuing support from the participants, particularly the SEC and influential leaders in the profession and the business community. It is important to note that constraints are also created by the integrity of the individuals appointed to the

FASB, the Board of Trustees, and FASAC, as well as those who donate funds to the Foundation and those who participate in the FASB's activities. If that integrity were lost or too severely compromised, the system would probably not function as well as it has.

Three Levels of Politics

In conducting its activities, the FASB encounters the need for political action on at least three levels:

- Among its seven members.
- Between itself and its constituencies.
- Between itself and the SEC.

On the first level, negotiation and compromise are essential to the development of a consensus on the issues related to a proposed accounting standard. Seldom do even two people agree on what the question is, much less its best answer. When reaching an agreement among four Board Members to get a majority vote, it is virtually always necessary that each of them give up something that he would otherwise prefer to be a part of the answer. Thus, each Board Member must enter deliberations on a project with an idea of which points are most important and least important; then, as the debate ensues, the struggle becomes one of attempting to preserve the most important, even if it means letting the others fall aside. This compromising is a critical part of politics.

On the second level, the Board must be responsive to the apparent positions of its constituent groups of statement users, statement preparers, and auditors. If the steps in the due process reveal that these groups do not agree with the Board's assessment of the situation, then it behooves the Board to find a compromise that is more likely to be acceptable. Although the independence of the Board allows it to act like an emperor, it would not be prudent to push that power to its limits except in very limited circumstances. The articles in the Prologue show how the FASB reacted to the input from the affected companies and others in the defeasance project.

On the third level, the Board has to acknowledge that the SEC has more power than the other groups, with the consequence that careful attention must be paid to the Commission's needs. After all, it would not be worth the effort to establish a standard that the Board Members knew would be unacceptable to the SEC. Thus, as described earlier in the chapter, it is important for the FASB to establish and maintain close communications with the SEC and to be responsive to the demands placed on the Commissioners in their own environment.

In summary, the answer to the question of whether the FASB is a political institution is a clear yes. This answer should be understood to mean that the FASB governs **by negotiation and compromise** rather than **by manipulative means**. On the other hand, it would be naive to believe that manipulative methods and motives never enter into the activities of the Board and its constituents.

The Implications of a Political Process

At this point, it is appropriate to observe three implications of the fact that accounting standards setting is a political process.

First, and perhaps most important, politics tend to make generally accepted accounting principles **logically inconsistent** because the consensus needed to resolve an issue will be shaped by those in power and how important the issues are to them. Thus, inconsistencies will appear between standards issued at different times, under different standards setters, and in different industry settings. One example of this type of inconsistency can be seen in the differences between Statement of Financial Accounting Standards 2 (SFAS 2), which requires all research and development costs to be expensed, and SFAS 86, which was issued 11 years later and requires capitalization of certain costs of developing computer software.

Because the FASB derives its authority from the SEC, and because the SEC derives its authority from the Congress and the president, there can be inconsistencies between standards issued under different national administrations. For example, disclosures of information about the effects of changing prices were required by SFAS 33, which was issued during the populist Carter administration. On the other hand, these provisions were rescinded by SFAS 82 and SFAS 89, which were issued during the deregulatory Reagan administration. Of course, other factors also contributed to the elimination of these requirements.

A second major implication of politics is found in the attitudes of constituents toward GAAP as they exist. Given the different interests and the need to compromise to reach a consensus, it is virtually certain that at least **someone will be unhappy with any rule**. It may even be true that **everyone** will be unhappy because so many compromises will have been reached. Because of this condition, the FASB (or any standards setter) must expect opposition on any issue that it attempts to resolve. Furthermore, it must have the institutional will to stand up to the opposition, or it will lose its capacity to bring about meaningful reform.

A third implication concerns the occurrence of change in GAAP. Given the dynamics of politics with its shifts in power and priorities, **it is inevitable that GAAP will change**. No one can count on a rule remaining in effect forever. On the other hand, **GAAP cannot be changed quickly**. Those who want to bring about change must muster their forces to get a project on an agenda and then keep it moving ahead to a satisfactory resolution against a stubborn opposition that will want to keep the change from taking place. In effect, change will happen, but not sudden change. This inertia is frustrating to those who would seek to reform practice, but it has the positive feature of creating stability in the social order of accounting.

SELECTED READINGS

AICPA. *Objectives of Financial Statements.* Report of the Study Group on the Objectives of Financial Statements. New York, 1973.

BEAVER, WILLIAM H. *Financial Reporting: An Accounting Revolution.* Englewood Cliffs, N.J.: Prentice-Hall, 1981.

CYERT, RICHARD M., and YUJI IJIRI. "Problems of Implementing the Trueblood Objective Report." *Studies on Financial Accounting Objectives,* supplement to *Journal of Accounting Research,* 1974, pp. 29–32.

GERBOTH, DALE L. "Research, Intuition, and Politics in Accounting Inquiry." *Journal of Accountancy,* July 1973, pp. 475–82.

JOHNSON, STEVEN B., and DAVID SOLOMONS. "Institutional Legitimacy and the FASB." *Journal of Accounting and Public Policy* 3 (1984), pp. 165–83.

SOLOMONS, DAVID. "The Politicization of Accounting." *Journal of Accountancy,* November 1978, pp. 65–72.

ZEFF, STEPHEN A. "The Rise of Economic Consequences." *Journal of Accountancy,* December 1978, pp. 56–63.

REVIEW QUESTIONS (including the Prologue)

1. List 10 key points illustrated by the news stories in the Prologue.

2. Why, in general, is financial accounting considered important?

3. How does financial accounting contribute to a smooth-running, efficient U.S. economy?

4. Many resources of an entity are generated internally through its own profitable activities. How does an entity acquire resources externally?

5. What mechanism is used in capital markets to allocate available resources among those competing for them?

6. Through what medium are providers of external resources matched with consumers of resources?

7. Why is much of the information for making capital markets decisions financial in nature?

8. Consumers and providers consider alternative sources and investments in capital markets. Decisions are reached and contracts entered into. Why is information the lifeblood of all rational decision making?

9. In order to make rational decisions, what do providers and consumers of capital need to know?

10. Identify several types and sources of financial information.

11. What is one major type of financial information that is prepared and distributed by corporations?

12. What presumably will happen to the economy if decisions in capital markets are made in light of useful financial information?

13. Identify five groups that have an interest in financial accounting and indicate the

reason for each group's interest. Are these groups' reasons for interest in financial accounting different?

14. Discuss the concepts of uniformity and comparability as they relate to financial accounting. Why are these concepts considered important in financial accounting?

15. How do financial accounting rules seeking uniformity affect users of financial accounting information? corporate management? auditors?

16. What term is used to describe the set of chosen rules and guidelines for preparing financial statements?

17. What mechanism has been established to resolve differences on which rule or guideline should be established for a particular problem in financial accounting?

18. The Financial Accounting Standards Board is the operating part of a three-part structure. What are the other parts?

19. What is the main role of the Financial Accounting Foundation?

20. How many trustees administer the FAF?

21. How are FAF trustees appointed?

22. What impact does the FAF have on the standards-setting work of the FASB?

23. What is the primary role of the Financial Accounting Standards Advisory Council (FASAC)?

24. In what year was the FASB founded?

25. Prior to the founding of the FASB, what groups were responsible for financial accounting rule making?

26. What authority does the FASB have in establishing generally accepted accounting principles? Can the FASB enforce GAAP? If not, who can?

27. Has the SEC ever indicated a desire for the FASB to establish GAAP? If so, how?

28. What other groups have added to the authority of the FASB and how?

29. What groups have added to the influence of the FASB even though they have not added to its authority?

30. The FASB follows a set of procedures collectively called the *due process*. Identify the process of the FASB *in general*.

31. According to Don Kirk, former FASB chairman, what kinds of issues are generally debated by the FASB?

32. Distinguish between the two common definitions of politics.

33. Discuss an alternative to standards setting by means of a political process.

34. How does the FASB's structure capture the advantages of both the participative and the emperor approach to standards setting?

35. List the three levels on which the FASB encounters the need for political action.

EXERCISES

1. The term *information* was used in this chapter and tends to be used extensively in accounting. What is "information"? What characteristics make information use-

ful? Is there a difference between information and data? Is information that might not be useful included in financial statements and footnotes? How could information that is not useful be included in financial statements and footnotes?

2. Identify three decisions that might be based on financial accounting information. Also, identify the financial accounting information relevant to the decisions. How can the Financial Accounting Standards Board identify the information needed in financial statements for decision making?

3. The controversy over accounting for the defeasance of debt was presented in the Prologue. Review the articles on defeasance and identify the organizations and people participating in the discussions and decisions. Also identify why each organization or person was participating.

4. A manager in your firm has been asked to present a short speech on an accounting controversy at a local business luncheon. The manager has asked you to assist in preparing the talk. You are to review relevant business publications such as *The Wall Street Journal* and *Business Week* to identify the following:

    a. A financial accounting topic that is "in the news."

    b. The importance of the topic to the financial statements (for example, defeasance of debt affected the debt position on the balance sheet and resulted in a gain on the income statement).

    c. The parties participating in discussions about the topic.

    d. The status of the accounting for the event.

    The manager has asked you to prepare a memo on your findings.

5. Identify three groups that you belong to and describe the political processes that are used to govern each group. An example of a group might be your accounting class.

2

The People and the Structure of the FASB

The structure of any organization should reflect its purpose. The FASB is no different in this respect, and its structure is intended to allow it to meet its goal of resolving controversial issues while providing for participation by a large number of interested parties. However, the task of designing the structure has occurred in the face of a paradox. On one hand, the Board must be **independent** of any *particular* constituent group in order to be relieved from pressure to provide standards that promote the interest of that group. On the other hand, the Board must remain **dependent** on *all* the groups in order to derive sufficient power from their endorsements to allow it to create authoritative answers. This dependence also encourages the members of the groups to participate in the FASB's due process procedures. This fine balance between independence and dependence is not easy to maintain; however, many observers feel that the FASB has been successful because it has balanced these opposing forces.

As described briefly in Chapter 1, the organization has these three components:

- **Financial Accounting Foundation**
- **Financial Accounting Standards Board**
- **Financial Accounting Standards Advisory Committee**

Each component has its own duties and accountabilities for performance; each also is subject to constraints that limit its ability to interfere with the others. By subdividing the responsibilities and limiting the powers, the designers produced a system that achieves the balance considered essential to the Board's success.[1]

Because so much of the FASB's activity involves the work of the **Research and Technical Activities Staff**, this chapter also explains its structure, personnel, and duties.

FINANCIAL ACCOUNTING FOUNDATION

The Foundation is the "parent" organization in the FASB's structure. Incorporated under the laws of Delaware as a nonprofit corporation, it qualifies as an institution "organized to operate exclusively for charitable, educational, scientific and literary purposes" under Section 501(c)(3) of the federal Internal Revenue Code. Because of the Foundation's nonprofit status, its income is exempt from taxation, and donations are deductible as charitable contributions on donors' tax returns. As justification for this tax treatment, the Foundation's certificate of incorporation includes this language:

> ...the purposes of the Corporation shall be to advance and to contribute to the education of the public, investors, creditors, preparers and suppliers of financial information, reporting entities and certified public accountants in regard to standards of financial accounting and reporting; to establish and improve the standards of financial accounting and reporting by defining, issuing and promoting such standards; to conduct and commission research, statistical compilations and other studies and surveys; and to sponsor meetings, conferences, hearings and seminars, in respect of financial accounting and reporting.[2]

The overall responsibility for these activities rests with the Foundation's 16-member **Board of Trustees**.

One major task of the trustees is raising the funds needed to finance the operations of the three organizations. It follows that the trustees are accountable to donors and the business community at large for the appropriate use of these funds.

A second major duty is the appointment of the members of the Financial Accounting Standards Board and the Financial Accounting Standards Advisory Council. The procedures used for this task and the qualifications of the appointees are discussed later in this chapter in the sections on the Board and the Council.

A third activity of the trustees is reviewing the performance of the FASB. As a result of such administrative reviews by the trustees' Structure Commit-

---

[1]The basic structure was designed by a special study group of the AICPA headed by Mr. Francis M. Wheat. The 1972 proposal of the Wheat Study Group was endorsed by the AICPA and other organizations, and implemented within a year.

[2]*Restated Certificate of Incorporation of the Financial Accounting Foundation,* as amended through June 29, 1984, section 3.

tee, a number of changes in Board procedures have been implemented. The following items are examples of these changes:

- Expanded use of Task Forces and scheduling of public hearings outside New York City. (Chapter 3 describes the nature and purposes of these steps in the due process procedures.)
- Broadened membership of the Board of Trustees, the FASB, and FASAC to be more representative of the constituent groups.[3]
- Expansion of the size of the Staff and the delegation of greater responsibilities to Staff members.
- Reduction of the number of assenting Members needed to approve a standard for publication from a two-thirds majority (five Board Members) to a simple majority (four Members).
- Virtual elimination of closed-door meetings of the FASB.[4]
- Expanded use of special meetings with constituents for the purpose of educating Board Members about highly specialized areas of practice.

None of these changes can be considered a radical reform of the basic structure created in 1973.

To maintain the Board's independence, the Foundation's review is limited to examining the FASB's efficiency and its ability to respond to the views of its constituencies. The trustees are not to interfere in or even attempt to influence the outcome of the standards-setting process. The Foundation's bylaws specifically state:

> . . . the Trustees shall not, by or in connection with the exercise of their power of approval over annual budgets or their periodic review of such operating and project plans, direct the FASB or GASB to undertake or to omit to undertake any particular project or activity or otherwise affect the exercise by the FASB or GASB of their authority, functions and powers in respect of standards of financial accounting and reporting.[5]

By this limitation, the separation of powers is at least nominally maintained. While this provision precludes the trustees from exerting direct influence on Board Members concerning accounting issues, the fact remains that trustees

---

[3]Under the structure initially established in response to the Wheat Study Group report, four of the seven FASB Members had to be CPAs. This provision may have reflected the concerns of the AICPA about relinquishing its 35 years of control over the establishment of accounting principles. The major factor that triggered the elimination of this rule was the investigation of the accounting profession by congressional subcommittees in the mid-1970s. A report prepared by one of the subcommittees expressed concerns that auditors had too much influence on standards setting and that statement preparers had too much influence on auditors.

[4]Prior to this change, virtually all deliberations among the Board Members were closed to the public, with the consequence that the constituencies were not as involved in the process. This change was also a result of the congressional hearings described in footnote 3.

[5]*Bylaws of the Financial Accounting Foundation,* as amended through June 29, 1984, chapter A, article 1-A, section 1.

control reappointment to the Board. Thus, it is at least theoretically possible that a Board Member might modify a position on an issue to assure reappointment; however, there is no evidence that such a result has ever occurred.

It is also possible that the Board's independence could be endangered if a particular constituency group were to gain control of the Foundation's Board of Trustees who would then select new Board Members who in turn would advocate that group's interests over the interests of others. Clearly, the greatest threat to the FASB would arise if this control were to rest with financial statement preparers because they are the group being regulated. This issue of whether preparers dominate the Board is discussed in more detail in the Epilogue.

The Trustees

The 16 trustees of the Foundation meet at least four times each year, usually once each quarter. The agenda for the meeting is publicly announced, and the meetings are open to public observers, except for deliberations on particularly sensitive matters, such as the evaluation of candidates for appointment (or reappointment) to the FASB and FASAC.

The trustees can serve no more than two terms of three years each. They select their own President, but the day-to-day administration is performed by a salaried Executive Vice President and Chief Administrative Officer. In 1987, the President was Mr. Rholan Larson, a practicing CPA from a regional firm, and the Executive Vice President was Mr. Joseph S. La Gambina.

Of the 16 trustees, 13 are formally elected to their positions by eight so-called Electors, who are the official members of the nonprofit corporation as required by Delaware laws. These individuals are in turn selected by the governing boards of eight sponsoring organizations. Each individual is either the senior elected official or the full-time executive director of the organization he or she represents. Although the Electors technically have the power to vote for any candidate for a trustee's position they wish, practice shows that they have merely approved the individuals nominated by the participating organizations.

The 13 elected trustees' positions are allocated as follows:

American Accounting Association . . . . 1 trustee
American Institute of CPAs . . . . 4 trustees
Financial Analysts Federation . . . . 1 trustee
Financial Executives Institute . . . . 2 trustees
National Association of Accountants . . . . 1 trustee
Securities Industry Association . . . . 1 trustee
Various governmental accounting groups . . . 3 trustees

The three remaining at-large positions are filled by individuals elected by the other trustees. In 1987, one of these trustees was a retired auditor and another was a commercial banker. The third trusteeship was not filled; however, a December 1986 report from the Special Committee of the Foundation stated that it "is to be filled by election of a high-level corporate executive."[6] If this recommendation is followed, it will give financial statement preparers four positions, and possibly five, if the banker is considered to be a preparer. To the authors, this decision is unfortunate because the trustees could have brought additional credibility and stature to the Foundation by the appointment of a nationally prominent leader from outside business, such as a former cabinet officer, a retired elected national official, or the president of a major university.

A Financial Perspective

To grasp the magnitude of the operations of the Foundation and the responsibilities of the trustees for raising funds, it is helpful to see these amounts from the financial statements included in the FAF's annual report for 1986 (all in millions):

	Total	FASB	GASB
Net contributions	$ 6.2	$ 4.7	$1.5
Publications (net of direct costs)	6.2	5.7	0.5
Total operating revenues	12.4	$10.4	$2.0
Income from investments	1.4		
Total revenues	$13.8		

Notice that half the Foundation's operating revenues come from donations, but that they constitute only 45 percent of the funds needed by the FASB.

Of the funds contributed to the FASB, 44 percent came from public accountants and 56 percent from what were identified in the annual report as "industrial companies, banks, and financial institutions." According to the Foundation's Executive Vice President, amounts contributed by individuals and organizations from the statement user constituency were "negligible." As with the mix of the Trustees, these measures may also raise the issue of whether the FASB is dominated by statement preparers.

The expenditures section of the financial statements shows that the FASB is clearly a labor-intensive operation because Board and Staff Member salaries and benefits consumed $7.4 million, or about 70 percent of the operating revenues.

The amount of income from investments was substantially increased from prior years (it was only $0.5 million in 1985).

The statement of financial position as of the end of 1986 reports working capital of $2.9 million, with only an additional $0.9 million invested in

---

[6]Financial Accounting Foundation, "Report of the Special Committee to the Board of Trustees," December 4, 1986, p. 18.

operating assets. In addition, there were $12.9 million of investments in the "Reserve Fund." With this much set aside, the Foundation could manage to operate for several years at a decreased level of contributions if one constituency or another decided to cut back its donations.

THE FINANCIAL ACCOUNTING STANDARDS BOARD

In the three-part structure, the FASB is the "action arm" in the sense that it is responsible for accomplishing the main task of setting accounting standards. Its structure (and the Staff's) is directed toward the achievement of these three tasks:

- Serving as the focal point for **research**.
- **Communicating** with constituents.
- **Resolving** financial accounting issues.

Board Members

The primary purpose for making the trustees responsible for fund raising is to help insulate the seven Board Members from the pressures associated with that task. This arrangement allows them to work full time on the issues and, importantly, to deal with them without concern for the effect of a standard on the constituents' willingness to contribute funds. Whether the system actually accomplishes that goal is a significant question; however, there is no systematic evidence that a Board Member has taken a position on a proposed standard because of the threat of withheld funds. As an item of anecdotal evidence of a related phenomenon, one of the authors participated in a 1984 conference in which the controller of Texaco stated that his company would withhold its donation to the Foundation if the FASB implemented its proposed accounting for pensions.

Other steps have been taken to help Board Members preserve their independence in fact and in appearance. In particular, they sever their relationship with their previous employers and become full-time employees of the Foundation. Their independence is also bolstered by the size of their annual salaries, which (in 1987) were $240,000, with the Chairman receiving an additional $60,000. This arrangement makes their situation far different from the one faced by members of the Accounting Principles Board, who received no compensation and remained affiliated with (and presumably under the influence of) their employers. To protect Board Members against one form of lobbying, they can accept only token gifts as a result of a speech or other public appearance, and any cash honoraria are turned over to the Financial Accounting Foundation. They must file a quarterly statement that discloses the nature and size of investments they hold. They are required to disqualify themselves from voting on issues in which there could be a conflict of interest concerning their investments or other conditions; however, no Board Member has ever done so.

Generally, a Board Member is appointed to a five-year term, with the possibility of reappointment for one additional term. If the initial appointment is for a partial term as a replacement for a Member who resigned, the individual is still eligible for two complete five-year terms.

In selecting Board Members, the trustees attempt to find individuals who possess a number of qualifying characteristics. For example, according to the 1986 report prepared by the Foundation's Special Committee, Board Members should have the following qualifications:[7]

1. **Knowledge of financial accounting and reporting.**
2. **High level of intellect applied with integrity and discipline.**
3. **Judicial temperament.**
4. **Ability to work in a collegial atmosphere.**
5. **Communication skills.**
6. **Awareness of the financial reporting environment.**
7. **Commitment to the FASB's mission.**

The Special Committee also considered whether there is a need for a formal requirement to maintain a balance among the Board Members in terms of the constituencies from which they come. Basically, the members of the committee determined that the background should be "secondary" to the qualities listed above, but they also recognized that

> a reasonable mix of backgrounds should be an important consideration in selecting members so as to ensure a realistic range of viewpoints and/or perspectives on the Board. It was recommended by the Review Committee and approved by the Board of Trustees in July 1985 that the trustees continue to seek a Board make-up which includes a mix of backgrounds of members who have had major experience in public accounting, in business or industry, as a user of financial information, and as an accounting educator (p. 4).

Essentially, the committee acknowledged that it is politically prudent to balance the membership for the Board to remain broadly supported and viable. Consequently, even before this recommendation, the trustees usually attempted to replace a retiring Board Member with another individual with a similar background. In 1985, this practice came under attack from some members of the statement preparer constituency who suggested very strongly that at least two and preferably three members of the Board should be preparers. This sort of criticism is to be expected from this group because its members are most constrained by the FASB's standards. However, it should be apparent that this pressure is directly contrary to the earlier quoted bylaw that restricts the Trustees from using their power to "affect the exercise by the FASB or GASB of their authority, functions and powers in respect of standards of financial accounting and reporting." It remains to be seen how

---

[7]Financial Accounting Foundation, "Report of the Special Committee to the Board of Trustees," December 4, 1986, pp. 15–18.

the trustees and the other constituents (including the SEC) will resist this pressure, ignore it, or submit to it.

Throughout this section of the chapter, there are short biographies of the Board Members who were expected to be serving in 1988.

The Chairman of the Board

The Chairman of the FASB is selected by the Board of Trustees and is given special responsibilities beyond those of other Board Members. In return for this designation and duties, he receives additional compensation. His most visible additional duty is to serve as the moderator of regular Board meetings and other sessions, such as public hearings. His less visible duties include the development and supervision of a number of administrative policies for Members of the Board and Staff. The Chairman also works with the trustees in developing the operating budget for the Board. In addition, he is the primary contact point between the FASB and the rest of the business community. As such, he is called on to make many speeches and to appear before congressional committees or in other settings in which the Board is to be officially represented.

The 1986 Report by the Foundation's Special Committee identified these leadership qualities that the Chairman should possess:

1. Ability to set a sensible course toward a reasonable objective (or multiple objectives) and to direct an organization in following that course.
2. Ability to inspire colleagues and subordinates to maximum effort.
3. Ability to mediate among conflicting claims on resources.
4. Ability to represent the organization effectively as public spokesman.
5. Ability to deal with the unique character of the FASB:
   a. To steer a diverse group of strong-minded individuals toward consensus.
   b. To be politically sensitive to current and potential problems and conflicting needs with regard to the SEC, Congress, other governmental units, and to the private sector constituencies.

Thus, the Committee recognized that it takes more than mere technical or executive ability to be a successful chairman.

When the authors asked Denny Beresford whether being the Chairman affects his ability to reach or express a stance on an issue, he stated that he prefers to "put his position on the table" in order to "try to influence other Board Members." Unlike his predecessor, who preferred to meet with the staff team after its members had talked with other Board Members in small group sessions, Denny said that he likes meeting with the others to understand more about their positions. With respect to his approach to running public Board meetings, it is his goal to have "real debate" instead of careful expression of predetermined points. By having more discussion, he says, some of the Board's "inefficiency can be eliminated."

Dennis R. Beresford **Age:** 48

Education: B.S., University of Southern California (Accounting)

Appointed to FASB: 1987

Denny graduated from USC in 1961 with a B.S. in public accounting. He then joined the staff of the Los Angeles office of Ernst & Whinney. His next 10 years provided him with a wide variety of clients, including companies in the electronics, aerospace, publishing, and banking industries. He especially enjoyed working on the audits of the L.A. Rams and California Angels. In 1971, Denny was transferred to the E&W national office in Cleveland, and shortly thereafter was made a partner. At the time of his appointment to the Board, he was National Director of Accounting Standards, a position that required him to draft his firm's responses to FASB discussion documents. He was no stranger to the Board's activities because he had served on FASAC for four years, was a member of the Income Tax project's task force, and was a charter member of the Emerging Issues Task Force. He considers the chairmanship to be the "culmination of everything I've been doing in my professional career."

Denny is married and has two children in college. His wife is an accomplished artist and photographer. In his time away from the office, he enjoys golf, mystery and spy novels, and his two golden retrievers.

Age: 57   **Victor H. Brown**

Education: B.S., Wharton (Accounting)
MBA, Wharton (Industrial Management)
Ph.D., Univ. of Buffalo (Economics)

Appointed to FASB: 1983

Vic Brown says he accepted a Board position as a public service opportunity offering a broadening experience. He feels his training matches up well with the requirements of the job. Vic was a member of FASAC for four years. He served on the FASB's Oil and Gas Task Force, and in the late 70s was chairman of the Committee on Corporate Reporting of the Financial Executives Institute. Early in his accounting career, Vic moved from the staff of a small public accounting firm in Philadelphia to the University of Buffalo faculty. Then, he joined Touche Ross in New York City, where he served as managing partner of the New York office and regional managing partner until he became the controller, later promoted to vice president, of Standard Oil of Indiana. Vic was executive vice president and chief financial officer of Firestone at the time of his appointment to the FASB.

**Raymond C.
Lauver**

Age: 58

Education: B.S., Susquehanna University (Accounting)

Appointed to FASB: 1984

Ray began his accounting career with Price Waterhouse in New York City after serving in the Army. He had a vast amount of experience with large companies in the audit practice of PW, followed by several years with the small business department of PW. In 1961, Ray transferred to technical services, working in more of a research than practice capacity for the firm analyzing accounting and audit reports and supporting policy development within the firm. Just prior to joining the Board, Ray was national director of accounting services for the firm.

In the standard-setting environment, Ray participated in PW activities with the Accounting Principles Board and was a member and chairman of the AICPA Accounting Standards Executive Committee. Ray gained familiarity with the Board by serving on its Advisory Council and the screening committee on emerging problems and as a member of FASB task forces on research and development and pensions.

As a bit of good natured self-depreciation, Ray indicated that he was selected to be an FASB Board member because of "lots of refusals by other people." Given his career, however, it is easy to see that he was selected for his many good qualities. He accepted the position "as a public service, not to do it better, not for money, but as a commitment to the profession."

FINANCIAL ACCOUNTING STANDARDS ADVISORY COUNCIL

The principal objective of the Financial Accounting Standards Advisory Council (FASAC) is to provide advice to the Board and the Staff. This advice is generally directed along two general lines. First, it concerns the priorities of projects that are either before the Board or that could come before it. Thus, FASAC can suggest that the Board move more quickly to get certain issues resolved or that it move more slowly on less pressing ones. Through its Agenda Advisory Committee (discussed in Chapter 3), FASAC can also suggest that new issues be added to the agenda.

The second area in which advice is offered concerns the suitability of the preliminary positions that the Board has developed in the projects on its agenda. The positions can be those that have been drawn only tentatively, or they can be those that have been expressed in an Exposure Draft (also discussed in Chapter 3). In this capacity, FASAC serves as a sort of sounding board to let the FASB know more about how it is doing and how it is perceived by the community at large.

Age: 63   **C. Arthur Northrop**

Education: B.S., Columbia University (Accounting)

Appointed to FASB: 1986

Art went to work for IBM in 1942 after graduating from Columbia. Over the next 41 years, he filled a number of different positions at IBM, including chief accountant, controller, and, finally, treasurer. Because of company policy, he "retired" upon reaching age 60, but certainly did not drop out or even slow down. He remained a consultant with the company, and was serving on the board of directors of Intel at the time he was appointed to the FASB. Art believes that he received the appointment because he spent his entire career as an accountant and because of his activities with the FEI's Committee on Corporate Reporting, which gave him experience in dealing with financial accounting standards issues and allowed him to participate in the Board's due process.

It can be seen, then, that FASAC fills the void left by the restriction that keeps the trustees from advising the Board on its tentative resolutions of the issues. However, FASAC has no responsibility for raising funds or being involved in any way in the administration of the FASB's activities.

There are approximately 30 members of FASAC, each of whom may be appointed by the Board of Trustees for as many as four consecutive one-year terms. Originally, it was thought that 20 members would be sufficient to attain the balance that was essential to providing well-rounded advice from all quarters; however, practice showed that more people wanted to serve and that their views could be efficiently heard. Consequently, the actual number has been higher than the minimum of 20 called for in the Rules of Procedure [Section II (C)]. Except for the Chairman, Council members receive no compensation for their services and their employers are generally expected to pay their travel and other expenses. In 1987, the Chairman was Paul Kolton, who was the chairman of the American Stock Exchange prior to taking office in 1978. His duties include arranging for the four quarterly meetings of the Council (which requires providing all members with adequate information about the Board's agenda), moderating the meetings, preparing plans and budgets for Council activities, preparing reports on those activities, and advising the trustees on the appointment of Council members. He is assisted by an Executive Director, Mr. Paul G. Simpson.

Like Board Members, Council members are selected with the objective of balancing views. To use Paul Kolton's word, the goal in appointing members is to obtain a "microcosm" of the business community that will be likely to keep the Board from failing to consider some significant constituent's views when it resolves an issue. The 1987 Council members have the following backgrounds:

	Number	Percent
Attorney	1	3.4
Banking	4	13.8
CPA (largest firms)	4	13.8
CPA (others)	2	6.9
Economist	1	3.4
Government	1	3.4
Healthcare	1	3.4
Insurance	1	3.4
Professors	2	6.9
Securities industry	3	10.3
Statement preparers ...	9	31.0

Again, the numbers suggest that the preparer constituency representation might be considered disproportionate.

Council Meetings

The Council meets once each quarter, usually in New York City. Each meeting is attended by most members of the Council as well as all Board Members. Council meetings are also attended by the Chief Accountant of the Securities and Exchange Commission, who was Mr. Clarence Sampson until his appointment as a Board Member in 1987. Although he is not a member, the Chief Accountant participates in the discussions and informs the FASAC

Robert J. Swieringa   **Age:** 44

Education: A.B., Augustana College
M.B.A., University of Denver
Ph.D., University of Illinois (Accounting)

Appointed to FASB: 1986

After completing his Ph.D., Bob joined the faculty of Stanford University, where he took over the courses that had been taught by Dr. Robert Sprouse. By coincidence, his appointment to the Board again made him the successor to Dr. Sprouse, who served on the FASB from 1973 through 1985. At the time that Bob was appointed to the FASB, he was a professor at Cornell University. When pushed to answer, he said that he believes that the most important reason for his selection is his research record. His colleagues have suggested that his honest and forthright friendliness probably had a great deal to do with it, too. Bob feels that teaching financial accounting in Cornell's MBA program gave him a user's perspective for evaluating the issues that come before the Board.

James J. Leisenring

Age: 47

Education: B.S., Albion College (Economics)
M.S., Western Michigan (Finance)

Appointed to FASB: 1987

A native of Michigan (and an avid Tigers fan), Jim brings an unusually diverse background to the FASB. After earning his master's degree, he taught finance at Western Michigan University for several years. He then joined a regional public accounting firm, where he was later made a partner, and served as the Director of Accounting and Auditing. He is not a newcomer to standards setting, as evidenced by the fact that he was the Chairman of the AICPA's Auditing Standards Board when he was appointed the Director of the FASB's Research and Technical Activities Staff in 1982. During the five years he served as the Director, he administered the staff, participated in Board discussions of the issues, made countless speeches, and was the Chairman of the Emerging Issues Task Force. His personality, intellect, energy, and infectious enthusiasm have made him an effective and popular administrator and spokesman for the Board in a wide variety of settings, ranging from college classrooms to Congressional hearings. When asked what went through his mind when he was offered the Member's position, he said, "I had a lot of misgivings about leaving the Director's job because of what it allowed me to do for the FASB, but the chance to have a direct effect on new Standards means that I can do even more for the Board and for financial reporting."

of the SEC's views on the issues. Staff members are present to answer questions about their projects. Occasionally, one or more FAF Trustees may attend.

Before the meeting, Council members are provided with a lengthy questionnaire that solicits responses to a number of questions concerning the Board's activities and potential activities. No votes are taken on any issues because the Council has no power to establish any policies. Rather, its purpose is to assure that the Board at least hears all the possible views on the questions it is trying to answer.

Some Council meetings are preceded by a meeting of the 7 members of the Agenda Advisory Committee, which is also attended by one Board Member as well as the Director and Assistant Director of the Research and Technical Activities Staff. The members of the Committee are selected by the FASAC Chairman, with an eye toward reflecting the mix of the interests of the constituencies. During the Council meeting, this Committee communicates its recommendations to the Board. Although the Committee has no power to add items to the agenda, its oversight role is important for keeping the FASB sensitive to the need to resolve controversial issues.

A. Clarence Sampson	**Age:** 58

A. Clarence Sampson

Age: 58

Education: B.S., University of Maryland (Accounting)

Appointed to FASB: 1988

A lifelong Marylander, Clarence had served 11 years as the Chief Accountant of the Securities and Exchange Commission in Washington, D.C., at the time of his appointment to the FASB. In that position, he advised the Commission and its staff on accounting policies to be used by publicly held corporations in their filings with the SEC. He was also responsible for the Commission's oversight of the FASB's activities and participated in discussions held at meetings of the Emerging Issues Task Force. Because Clarence was appointed as the acting Chief Accountant in 1976 and was confirmed in the position in 1978, he helped create and maintain the regulatory climate that allowed the FASB to develop and succeed as a private sector standards setting body. Prior to succeeding Sandy Burton in 1976, he had already been on the SEC's staff for 17 years. Before that, he was an auditor for the U.S. Air Force and practiced public accounting with Arthur Young in Washington. In addition to his years as what is generally considered to be the most powerful accountant in the country, Clarence brings to the FASB a universally held reputation as a thoughtful and articulate man of integrity. Despite his accomplishments, he is a soft-spoken and approachable person who is not only respected but very well liked.

RESEARCH AND TECHNICAL ACTIVITIES STAFF

In simplest terms, the duty of the 40 to 50 members of the Research and Technical Activities (RTA) Staff is to do whatever is needed to facilitate the work of the FASB and its Members. Among the specific tasks of the Staff are:

- Researching the issues at all stages in a project.
- Communicating with constituents.
- Facilitating communication among Board Members.
- Preparing preliminary proposals for Board deliberations.
- Preparing summaries of Board meetings.
- Drafting publications, including discussion documents and final pronouncements (described in Chapter 3).
- Analyzing written and oral comments from the constituencies.
- Distributing informal implementation guidance.
- Speaking and otherwise representing the FASB.
- Other public relations activities.

Like Board Members, Staff members are full-time employees of the FASB. With the exception of those participating in the various "fellow" programs discussed below, Staff members must sever their relationships with their previous employers to provide at least the appearance of independence, if not independence in fact. All Staff members must file a quarterly statement of their investments and are subject to the same prohibitions on their investment activity that apply to Board Members. Furthermore, Staff members generally do not serve on committees of professional organizations to avoid an appearance of conflict of interest.

Organizational Structure of the Staff

The nature of the Board's work has caused the Staff to operate without a traditional hierarchical structure. Specifically, the key element in the Board's activity is the **project**, and the Staff is assigned to project teams under the direction of a **Project Manager**. Included among the team members might be those from higher, equal, and lower levels. For example, Project Manager A might work for Project Manager B on one project as a consultant, but Project Manager B might work for Project Manager A on another. Each project team is assigned a **Senior Technical Advisor** and a variety of professional and clerical personnel, including an **Assistant Project Manager**, a **Technical Associate**, and a **Project Administrative Assistant**.

Given the nature of the work and the pressures that accompany it, Staff members tend to be highly mobile and energetic individuals. Resignations occur frequently, and new positions are filled quickly. This turnover is not a sign of instability but rather of the qualifications of the employees and the nature of the institution. A measure of continuity is provided by the presence of a group of long-term members, while special expertise is provided by those who stay for relatively short periods of time.

The Director of RTA

The RTA Staff is headed by a Director who (at the suggestion of the trustees' Structure Committee in the late 1970s) holds equal status with Board Members. Specifically, the Director has the same salary as a Board Member, is seated at the Board meeting table, and participates in the discussions of the issues. In late 1987, the Director's position was temporarily vacant following Jim Leisenring's appointment to the Board.

The Director is selected by the Chairman of the FASB and is given the responsibility for seeing that the Staff carries out its duties. Included with the responsibility is the authority to hire and fire other Staff members. The Director often helps Staff members in selecting strategies for developing a consensus on a project and occasionally participates in the private Staff meetings that take place with Board Members before a public meeting.

Leisenring chose to be very active in the public relations activities of the FASB, particularly as a representative to or a speaker for meetings of constituent associations. For example, he delivered 23 speeches to different groups in 1986.

Dr. J. T. Ball, Assistant Director of RTA, has primary responsibility for the general supervision of **Implementation and Practice Problem** projects. These projects involve more narrow issues that can be resolved with less due process and more quickly than **Major Projects**.[8] Prior to joining the FASB at its founding in 1974, J.T. was a Research Associate at the AICPA, where he produced more than 200 Interpretations of Accounting Principles Board Opinions.

There are two **Senior Technical Advisors**, Mr. Jules Cassell and Dr. Reed K. Storey. Reed was Director of Research at the AICPA until 1974 and played a key role in the operation of the Accounting Principles Board. One or the other serves as a consultant for every major project team and is called on for advice about technical, theoretical, or political considerations.

Project Managers

In many respects, the **Project Managers** are the main workhorses of the FASB staff. In a sense, they are analogous to the middle-level of management in typical corporate structures. Their compensation is comparable to the amount received by managers or new partners in public accounting firms. In 1987, their annual salaries ranged from $65,000 to $105,000.

One of their important responsibilities is to serve as go-betweens in several relationships. First, they serve as the main contact between the Board Members and the Staff. Second, as seen in the Prologue, they serve as the primary contact between the Board and the business community, particularly the press.

Perhaps the Project Managers' most difficult task is serving as the interface between Board Members in the process of developing a consensus on the issues. Specifically, the Project Manager attempts to find the compromises that will develop a sufficiently large consensus to allow a pronouncement to be issued. In doing so, the Project Manager goes between different Board Members, attempting to negotiate an acceptable position for as many of them as possible. This arrangement is generally preferable to having the Board Members deal with each other because they do not have to reveal to each other what concessions they are willing to make. On the other hand, it often makes the Project Manager's job more like diplomacy than accounting and is frequently frustrating.

The backgrounds of Project Managers are varied. Many of them come from public accounting; however, it is risky for them to interrupt their careers

---

[8]Examples of Implementation and Practice Problem (IPP) projects include the Defeasance project described in the Prologue and Accounting for Nonrefundable Loan Fees. Examples of major projects include the Conceptual Framework, Accounting for Financial Instruments, and Accounting for Income Taxes.

Joan Amble

Age: 34

Education: B.S., Pennsylvania State University; Graduate work at University of California at Los Angeles

Joined FASB Staff: 1984

Joan came onto the FASB staff with an unusually varied background that included experience in industry, academia, and public accounting. After graduating from Penn State (as a classmate of Rod Redding's), she first worked for Honeywell Corporation, but soon left to enroll in the Ph.D. program at UCLA, where she completed all requirements but her dissertation. While in graduate school, she worked with Professor John Buckley on several journal articles, which helped her develop her research and writing skills. She left Los Angeles to join the Ernst & Whinney office in Winston-Salem, North Carolina, and was then transferred to the Stamford office. The FASB became aware of her accounting and communication skills firsthand when she was E&W's manager for the annual audit of the Financial Accounting Foundation! When considering the job offer from the Board, she decided that a position on the staff would give her the opportunity to work with and learn from some of the most successful accounting professionals. While at the Board, she has been assigned to the Pensions project, and was the primary author of SFAS 88. During the summer of 1987, Joan took a leave from her project manager's position for the birth of her second child.

because of the difficulty of returning to their previous positions without having lost continuity. Others have come from private accounting or from teaching positions, and several have been promoted from lower Staff levels. As an insight into the types of people who fill this position, additional information is provided above and on the next page about two Project Managers, Mrs. Joan Amble and Mr. Halsey Bullen.

Fellow Positions

The FASB also has a "fellow" program to bring in Staff members for relatively short appointments for fixed terms. These programs provide the Board with special expertise and some fresh energy. Furthermore, the various programs lay a foundation for a network of leaders in the profession who have an intimate and useful knowledge of the purposes, processes, people, and politics of the Board.

Halsey Bullen

Age: 42

Education: A.B., Dartmouth College;
M.B.A., Stanford University

Joined FASB Staff: 1983

When Halsey accepted his Project Manager's position, he was coming home because he had grown up in Old Greenwich, Connecticut, the next town over from the Board's headquarters in Stamford. After graduating from Dartmouth, he served in the U.S. Navy as a Supply Corps officer on a destroyer. His next stop was the headquarters of Pepsico, but he soon left there for Stanford, where he studied accounting under none other than Dr. Robert Sprouse, who was a member of the FASB from its beginnings in 1973 through 1985. One of Dr. Sprouse's class projects required Halsey to develop his own conceptual framework and then use it to solve several accounting issues. The assignment came back to haunt him because his first project at the Board was to develop Statement of Financial Accounting Concepts No. 5, the document that marked the end of the Recognition and Measurement phase of the FASB's Conceptual Framework project. Between Stanford and Stamford were 10 years in the San Francisco office of Deloitte Haskins & Sells. He is currently heading up the massive FASB project on Financial Instruments, which is expected to last well into the 1990s. When the authors asked him whether he plans to be around to see the end of the project, he smiled and said that his experience has taught him that "just about anything is possible."

Each year, several **practice fellows** from CPA firms come to the FASB for two-year terms. Most of them are on leave from the so-called Big Eight firms.[9] This dominance is not planned, but merely reflects the fact that a larger firm is more capable of absorbing the loss of the fellow's services for two years and of using the special knowledge that he or she gains at the FASB. To use their practical experience and to allow them to see a project through to its conclusion, practice fellows are typically assigned to Implementation and Practice Problem projects. Virtually all fellows have been promoted to partner after their service, and some have continued to work with the Board as representatives or spokespersons for their firms.

Occasionally, an **industry fellow** will come to the FASB from a corporate setting to provide some particular expertise. The presence on the Staff of a person with this background helps assure members of the preparer constituency that the Staff has some balance in its experience that should lead to balance in its deliberations and pronouncements.

Faculty fellows come from university teaching positions, usually with

---

[9]These firms are the largest in the United States: Arthur Andersen & Co.; Arthur Young & Company; Coopers & Lybrand; Deloitte Haskins & Sells; Ernst & Whinney; Peat Marwick Main & Co.; Price Waterhouse; and Touche Ross & Co.

sufficient prior development to justify the interruption of their academic career paths. Because of their training and interests, faculty fellows have typically been associated with the Conceptual Framework project or with projects requiring extensive research, such as the Accounting for Changing Prices project. There is usually only one faculty fellow on the Staff at any given time.

Graduate interns serve one year and come directly to the FASB after earning a degree but before beginning their professional careers. The individuals selected may have either a bachelor's degree or a master's degree. Approximately four interns are selected each year from nominees provided in response to invitations. Interns have been appointed from the following schools:

- Albion
- California at Berkeley
- Central Washington
- Colorado
- Illinois
- Nebraska
- Notre Dame
- Seattle
- Utah
- Wisconsin at Eau Claire
- Bucknell
- Central Michigan
- Clemson
- Florida State
- Louisiana State
- North Carolina
- Ohio State
- Southern California
- Virginia
- Wisconsin at Madison

Typically, the interns have taken positions with public accounting firms or continued their schooling upon completion of their terms.

The accompanying sidebar gives a short biography of Mr. Neal McGrath, who was a practice fellow from 1985 to 1987.

Neal McGrath

Age: 38

Education: B.S., University of Northern Alabama

Joined FASB Staff: 1985

After graduating from UNA, Neal moved to Atlanta as a staff accountant for Ernst & Whinney. During his 11 years there, his clients included several manufacturers, retailers, and the Coca Cola Company. As a memento, he keeps a Coke bottle on his shelf with lettering in Chinese that came from the first batch manufactured for distribution in the People's Republic. He was nominated for the Fellow's position out his region of E&W, and was one of two from the firm selected by the FASB in 1985. He took the job as an opportunity "to do something new," and found it a great opportunity. His main area of activity was as administrator of the Emerging Issues Task Force. When his term was up in June 1987, Neal returned to Atlanta as E&W's newest audit partner.

The Washington Office

In addition to its activities in Stamford, the Board operates an office in Washington, D.C., to maintain contact with Congress and various regulatory bodies concerned with financial reporting. For example, the FASB representative establishes relationships with and follows the activities of the SEC, the Federal Home Loan Bank Board, the Internal Revenue Service, the Interstate Commerce Commission, and the Small Business Administration. Furthermore, any congressional hearings or other matters related to the FASB's work are monitored. Another important purpose of the office is to help assure that the leadership of these government agencies fully understand the nature and mission of the FASB. The representative in the Washington office is Mrs. Patricia Pride.

APPENDIX
Predecessors of the FASB

The Committee on Accounting Procedure

In 1938, the Committee on Accounting Procedure (CAP) was formed by the American Institute of Accountants (now the American Institute of Certified Public Accountants). It was created primarily in response to the SEC's issuance of Accounting Series Release 4, which established that accounting principles used in filings with the SEC had to have "substantial authoritative support" in order to be considered generally accepted.[10]

During its existence, the committee generally had around 20 members, all of whom were members of the AIA. They all served on a part-time basis, and none of them were paid for their services.

The CAP did not have the broadly based authority that has been granted to the FASB. In fact, its pronouncements were not even binding on members of the AIA, who could consider alternative practices to be acceptable in some circumstances. Nonetheless, its publications were considered helpful guidance.

During its 21-year life, the CAP issued 51 *Accounting Research Bulletins* on a variety of subjects. ARB 43 was issued in 1953 as a codification, with some modifications, of the preceding bulletins. To the extent that it has not been amended or superseded by subsequent pronouncements, ARB 43 is still widely influential.

Because it lacked authority, the CAP generally was unable to be definitive in its pronouncements. In dealing with inventories, for example, ARB 43 says

---

[10]The CAP had its own predecessor body, dating back to 1917, when the AIA cooperated with the Federal Reserve Board in developing a booklet called *Approved Methods for the Presentation of Balance Sheet Statements,* which described basic accounting principles.

only that "A major objective of accounting for inventories is the proper determination of income through the process of matching appropriate costs against revenues." This statement lacks operational guidance without a specification of what constitutes "proper determination" or "appropriate costs." Similarly, ARB 43 says that "it is perhaps in some circumstances permissible to show stock of a corporation held in its own treasury as an asset" but does not describe what those circumstances are or the rationale that supports this treatment.

Despite these weaknesses, Accounting Research Bulletins are recognized by the FASB as GAAP in its Rules of Procedure [Section III(K)] except when they have been specifically superseded. The SEC Accounting Series Release that endorsed the FASB's pronouncements also acknowledges Accounting Research Bulletins as acceptable for filings.

Because the CAP was entirely within the AICPA and consisted solely of individuals who belonged to the Institute, it lacked the broad power base that the FASB has developed. Moreover, locating the rule-making authority (however limited) within the auditing profession may have led to solutions that tended to address auditor's needs to the detriment of the interests of others. For example, because auditors need to reduce the risks of making incorrect judgments, they generally prefer such common practices as the use of cost-based measures, the application of systematic allocations, and reliance on transactions as events critical to the recognition of income (unless income is to be reduced). It is legitimate to debate whether such conservative practices help or hinder users and preparers of financial statements; however, that question cannot be resolved in this setting.

The CAP was dissolved in 1959 and replaced by another AICPA committee, described below.

The Accounting Principles Board

Like its predecessor, the CAP, the Accounting Principles Board (APB) was a committee of the AICPA. It was established in 1959 and existed until 1973. The APB was created as a result of a general concern within the Institute that the CAP was simply not working well. One frequently cited reason was the lack of systematic research assistance for the CAP's members. Specifically, the CAP shared its staff with a large number of other AICPA committees. There was also concern about the CAP's authority because none of its members was authorized by his firm to describe its official positions on the issues; rather, each member was supposed to describe a more-or-less personal view.

The APB was created to deal with these apparent weaknesses. It was given a full-time research staff of six individuals and a Director of Accounting Research. This position was initially filled by Dr. Maurice Moonitz, who was succeeded by Paul Grady, who in turn was followed by Dr. Reed K. Storey, now Senior Technical Advisor on the FASB Staff.

In its first few years, members of the APB were predominantly the most senior partners of major accounting firms (the Board always included a representative from each of the Big Eight). The strategy in having such high level members was to derive authority for the Board's pronouncements from the authority of its members. However, most of these members did not commit as much time as the Board's work demanded, and a different solution was implemented. The chosen answer was to use slightly less senior personnel and have the AICPA governing council give authority to the Board's pronouncements by requiring AICPA members to specifically identify the effects of any departure from APB pronouncements in the auditor's opinion accompanying the client's financial statements.

In response to a complaint that the CAP did not have a consistent approach to solving accounting problems, the APB was initially given the task of developing a set of "postulates" (or basic concepts) to provide guidance for the settling of issues. This project led to the publication of Accounting Research Studies Nos. 1 and 3 (the former was written by Maurice Moonitz and the latter by Moonitz and Robert Sprouse, who was a Member of the FASB from 1973 through 1985). Both studies were rejected in APB Statement No. 1 as "too radically different from present generally accepted accounting principles to be acceptable at this time." Subsequently, other attempts to develop such underlying postulates were published, including the AICPA's Accounting Research Study No. 7 by Paul Grady, in 1965 and APB Statement No. 4 in 1970. None of these efforts produced results that were particularly helpful to the APB. Despite the struggles in this area, similar goals were established for the FASB's Conceptual Framework project, which is discussed in Chapter 5.

During its 14-year life, the APB issued 31 authoritative "Opinions," which the FASB also acknowledged in its Rules of Procedure as creating GAAP to the extent that they were not superseded or amended. The Opinions were generally more definitive than the CAP's Accounting Research Bulletins, largely because of the authority passed to the APB by the AICPA Council. It also issued four nonauthoritative "Statements."

The APB was dissolved in 1973, several months after the FASB was created. While there are many causes for its demise, perhaps the most significant was the lack of a broadly based mandate that would establish its authority. It is important to note that the SEC never did formally endorse the APB as a source of authority while it existed, although its pronouncements were so endorsed in ASR 150.

The APB also had a number of structural weaknesses, particularly its relatively large size (it started with 20 members, increased to 21, fell back to 18, and had only 17 in 1973) and the fact that its members served on a part-time basis. Furthermore, the members were not perceived as being independent of their firms or, in the case of the auditor members, the clients of their firms. In order to avoid these weaknesses, the FASB was given a smaller size and its members were made independent of their previous employers.

SELECTED READINGS

AICPA. "The FASB's Second Decade." *Journal of Accountancy,* November 1983, pp. 86–96, December 1983, pp. 94–102.

FASB. "Facts about FASB." [New edition released each year.]

MEYER, P. E. "The APB's Independence and Its Implications for the FASB." *Journal of Accounting Research,* Spring 1974, pp. 188–96.

ZEFF, STEPHEN A. "A Chronology of Significant Developments in the Establishment of Accounting Principles in the United States, 1926–1972." *Journal of Accounting Research,* Spring 1972, pp. 217–27.

————. "Some Junctures in the Evolution of the Process of Establishing Accounting Principles in the USA: 1917–1972." *Accounting Review,* July 1984, pp. 447–68.

REVIEW QUESTIONS

1. What is the intent of the structure of the FASB?
2. List the three components of the entire FASB organization.
3. Discuss the three primary activities of the Financial Accounting Foundation.
4. What limitations are placed on the activities of the FAF and what is the purpose of those limitations?
5. Provide some examples of changes that have occurred in the practices of the FASB as a result of the FAF's review procedures.
6. Identify some of the organizations that provide trustees to serve on the FAF.
7. What percentages of the donations to the FASB come from preparers of financial statements, auditors, and users of financial statements?
8. To what three tasks is the structure of the FASB directed?
9. What steps have been taken to help Board Members preserve their independence?
10. How long may a Board Member serve?
11. What characteristics might qualify a candidate to be a Board Member?
12. Identify some of the duties that the Chairman of the Board performs in addition to the duties performed by other Board Members.
13. What is the sole objective of the Financial Accounting Standards Advisory Council? Identify the two areas that the Council generally addresses in meeting this objective.
14. How many members serve on FASAC? How long do they serve? What salary are they paid? What are their backgrounds?
15. In addition to FASAC regular members and Board Members, who attends all FASAC meetings and what is his role?
16. Identify some of the tasks carried out by the Research and Technical Activities Staff of the FASB.
17. Discuss the role and status of the Director of the Research and Technical Activities Staff.

18. Identify the positions comprised by the second level of the Research and Technical Activities Staff and discuss the primary responsibilities of the positions.

19. Discuss the qualifications and responsibilities of a Project Manager.

20. What is the purpose of the "fellow" programs of the FASB? Identify the various types of fellows who participate in the program.

21. Discuss the responsibilities of the Washington, D.C., office of the FASB.

22. What action caused the formation of the Committee on Accounting Procedures?

23. Indicate the type of pronouncement that the CAP issued and discuss the authority of the CAP.

24. What is the content of ARB 43 and what is its present status?

25. Why was the Accounting Principles Board established?

26. What were the official pronouncements of the APB? What is their status today?

27. What factors led to the dissolution of the APB?

EXERCISES

1. For the past year, you have served as a trustee on the Financial Accounting Foundation. Today, you received a phone call from the chairman of the board of a major corporation who is concerned about the possible reappointment of an FASB Member who has consistently taken stands on standards that have resulted in lower earnings for the corporation. What factors would you consider in responding to the chairman? Prepare a brief reply.

2. The Structure Committee of the Financial Accounting Foundation thought it important to reduce the number of assenting Members of the FASB needed to approve a standard from *five* Members (a two-thirds majority) to *four* Members (a simple majority).

   a. Discuss arguments for and against going from a *five*-Member to a *four*-Member requirement.

   b. The Board now has seven Members. Discuss the size of the Board and the advantages and disadvantages of increasing or decreasing it. Recall that both of the FASB's predecessors, the CAP and APB, were larger groups.

3. Assume that you are a Board Member of the FASB. A good friend and former classmate of yours is now the chief financial officer for a major corporation. He has asked you to attend an annual retreat that his corporation holds in Bermuda to update corporate executives and to plan corporate strategies. You would speak to the group for about 30 minutes following dinner, on whatever contemporary accounting topic you considered useful to the audience. All of your expenses would, of course, be paid by the corporation. It is known to you that the outcome of an accounting issue presently under study by the Board could have an adverse effect on your friend's corporate financial statements. Will you accept or not accept, and why?

4. As a senior accounting major, you have expressed an interest in being an FASB graduate intern. Prepare a statement of what you would gain from this experience. Assume that the statement is one of the criteria that the FASB will use in selecting interns.

5. This exercise requires class participation and simulates the process by which an FASB Project Manager builds a Board consensus. Assume that an issue being addressed by the Board appears to have four potential solutions—A, B, C, and D. You are to specify which of these four alternatives you consider (1) strongly preferred, (2) acceptable but not preferred, (3) barely acceptable, and (4) not acceptable. You must assign each alternative a different ranking. One member of your class, serving as "project manager" will ask two randomly selected members of the class for their rankings. See if you can identify a consensus based on these rankings. Then, add a third member's ranking and again try to reach an agreement on the alternative you would select. You may repeat this process under several different "project managers."

3

The FASB's Due Process

The term *due process* is used in several different settings to describe the steps used to assure that an administrative matter is given the careful consideration necessary to adequately protect the interests of those involved. Thus, individuals accused of crimes cannot be convicted without having the allegations heard through a series of due process procedures. Similar concepts are applied in labor relations disputes and in legislative activities.

The Financial Accounting Standards Board also uses a set of due process procedures to assure that the interests of its constituents are considered in the development of accounting standards and other pronouncements. In carrying out these procedures, the FASB attempts to accomplish the following five broad goals:

- ☐ Discovery of an accounting problem.
- ☐ Identification of the accounting issues underlying the problem.
- ☐ Identification of alternative positions on those issues.
- ☐ Evaluation of those alternatives.
- ☐ Selection of the preferred alternative.

These goals are achieved through a set of procedures described later in the chapter.

Due process is considered essential, not only because it produces a systematic approach to problem solving, but also because it creates an environment in which the constituents and other members of the business community can feel that they have had an opportunity to affect the outcome. Even though a group may not agree with the FASB pronouncement, its members can have confidence that their needs were at least addressed and not completely disregarded.

This chapter contains the following sections on the FASB's procedures:

- The final pronouncements issued by the FASB.
- The steps in the overall process.
- The FASB's public relations activities.
- Participating in the FASB's due process procedures.

THE FINAL PRONOUNCEMENTS ISSUED BY THE FASB

The first step toward the FASB's goal of establishing generally accepted accounting principles was taken soon after its founding with its endorsement of the pronouncements of its predecessor bodies.[1] It has continued to establish GAAP by using its own pronouncements, including many revisions of earlier documents. The following four types of documents have been issued:

- ☐ **Statements of Financial Accounting Standards**
- ☐ **Interpretations**
- ☐ **Statements of Financial Accounting Concepts**
- ☐ **Technical Bulletins**

Each of these types is discussed below.

Statements of Financial Accounting Standards

Because of the AICPA's Ethics Rule 203 and similar regulations of state societies and state boards of public accountancy, a Statement of Financial Accounting Standards (SFAS) unambiguously creates generally accepted principles that must be complied with. Specifically, a CPA cannot state in an auditor's opinion that a client's financial statements are in compliance with GAAP if they are not in compliance with all SFASs. As mentioned in Chapter 1, a rarely invoked exception to this rule applies if compliance would produce misleading information in the financial statements. According to the SEC's Financial Reporting Release No. 1 (as originally stated in Accounting Series Release No. 150, issued in 1973), a SFAS is binding on preparers registering with the SEC and on their auditors.

As of the date that this book went to press (Fall 1987), 93 standards had been issued.

Specification of an accounting principle in a SFAS does not necessarily mean that the underlying problem was pervasive among most (or even several) sectors of the economy. Although many Standards have affected a large number of companies in different industries (such as the standards that

---

[1]FASB Rules of Procedure (as amended in 1985), Section III(K).

govern accounting for research and development expenditures, reporting of segment information, accounting for contingencies, accounting for leases, and accounting for pensions), many others have been highly specialized in the sense that they have attempted to solve narrow problems or problems arising in only a specific industry (such as the standards that govern accounting for the tax effects of United Kingdom stock relief, accounting for railroad track structures, and accounting for motion-picture companies). The length of standards has also varied substantially, ranging from only a few pages to over a hundred pages.

The extent of the due process procedures applied to a Standard varies significantly from situation to situation. Some projects go through many steps and others fewer. However, all final Standards must be preceded by the issuance of an Exposure Draft, which is described in the next major section of the chapter. According to the FASB's Rules of Procedure, a standard can be issued only after a majority of Board Members votes in favor of its issuance.

Interpretations

By the same authorities that apply to the Statements of Financial Accounting Standards, FASB Interpretations also create GAAP. According to the Board's Rules of Procedure [Section III(H)(3)], the purpose of Interpretations is "to clarify, explain, or elaborate on" an existing SFAS, an APB Opinion, or a CAP Accounting Research Bulletin "as an aid to its understanding." Because of their limited nature, Interpretations pass through a less extensive set of due process procedures than the one used for a SFAS. Specifically, preliminary positions are not widely exposed to the constituencies with an Exposure Draft. Instead, they are merely presented to FASAC and highly interested parties for a review period of not less than 15 days. In practice, the time of exposure has never been less than 30 days. Like a SFAS, an Interpretation is issued only after a majority of Board Members vote in favor of its issuance.

As of July 1987, 38 Interpretations had been issued. None have been issued recently. Evidence of their rarity is provided by the fact that Interpretation No. 36 was issued in October 1981, No. 37 in July 1983, and No. 38 in August 1984.

Examples of Interpretations include the following:

- No. 16: "Clarification of Definitions and Accounting for Marketable Equity Securities That Become Nonmarketable" (an Interpretation of SFAS 12)
- No. 27: "Accounting for a Loss on a Sublease" (an Interpretation of APB Opinion No. 30 and SFAS 13)
- No. 34: "Disclosure of Indirect Guarantees of Indebtedness of Others" (an Interpretation of SFAS 5)

Although allowed by the Rules of Procedure, no Interpretation of a Statement of Financial Accounting Concepts has ever been issued.

Statements of Financial Accounting Concepts

Unlike Statements of Financial Accounting Standards, Statements of Financial Accounting Concepts are not intended to create GAAP and they are not included under the SEC's Financial Reporting Release 1, the AICPA's Ethics Rule 203, or similar rules issued by state societies of CPAs or State Boards of Public Accountancy.

According to the Rules of Procedure, there are three purposes for issuing a SFAC: (1) to guide the FASB in its standards-setting work, (2) to guide practicing accountants in dealing with issues not resolved in the authoritative literature, and (3) to help educate nonaccountants. As discussed in Chapter 5, it is not clear whether these goals have been served by the Conceptual Framework or whether they even could have been.

Despite their non-GAAP status, SFACs were taken through extensive due process procedures because of their significant implications on the direction of the development of GAAP in the future. The steps included Discussion Memoranda, public hearings, and Exposure Drafts, as well as others.

The titles of the six existing statements are:

No. 1 Objectives of Financial Reporting for Business Enterprises
No. 2 Qualitative Characteristics of Accounting Information
No. 3 Elements of Financial Statements of Business Enterprises
No. 4 Objectives of Financial Reporting by Nonbusiness Organizations
No. 5 Recognition and Measurement in Financial Statements of Business Enterprises
No. 6 Elements of Financial Statements—a replacement of FASB Concepts Statement No. 3 (incorporating an amendment of FASB Concepts Statement No. 2)

The six concepts statements and the Conceptual Framework project are discussed in more detail in Chapter 5.

Technical Bulletins

Like a Concepts Statement, a Technical Bulletin (TB) issued by the FASB does *not* officially create GAAP; however, Bulletins are important for helping practicing accountants deal with pressing implementation problems. The issues addressed in TBs are neither pervasive nor particularly controversial; rather, they are usually troublesome to only a relatively small number of accountants.

According to the policies of the FASB, a TB is issued when:

- The guidance [in the TB] is not expected to cause a major change in accounting practice for a significant number of entities.
- The administrative cost that may be involved in implementing the guidance is not expected to be significant to most affected entities.

• The guidance does not conflict with a broad fundamental principle or create a novel accounting practice.[2]

Because of this restricted nature, only limited due process procedures are applied to TBs. They are usually distributed to only a few parties who are considered by the Staff to be likely to be interested in the problem. A proposed TB is always circulated to at least some members of the Emerging Issues Task Force (the duties of this group are discussed later in this chapter and in the Epilogue), FASAC, the Accounting Standards Executive Committee of the AICPA, and the Committee on Corporate Reporting of the Financial Executives Institute. Generally, no more than 400 copies of a proposed TB are distributed, whereas the Board often distributes many thousands of copies of the Exposure Drafts of a new SFAS.

Unlike the situation for other types of pronouncements, Board Members do not formally vote for or against the contents of a Technical Bulletin. However, if the discussion of the TB at a public Board meeting reveals that a majority of the Members object to its issuance, it will not be issued. The objections can be based on a disagreement with the proposed solution to the problem, an opinion that the problem should be covered by another type of pronouncement, or any other reason that a Board Member cares to raise.

The practice of issuing TBs began in 1979 as a result of concern with informal implementation advice requested in telephone or written inquiries from individuals who were trying to apply Standards and Interpretations. Because the same problems were raised in many inquiries, it was decided to make the advice more formal so it could be indexed in the authoritative literature and thus be more widely applied. Nineteen TBs were issued in 1979 as the Staff dealt with a backlog of problems that had been addressed over the preceding years. After that date, TBs were relatively uncommon. However, as a result of recommendations from a Timely Guidance Task Force of business leaders, the FASB decided in 1983 to use the TB as a way of getting guidance to financial accountants quickly and cheaply. Briefly, the Task Force determined that a number of problems deserved authoritative answers but were not sufficiently widespread or urgent to justify the cost and effort of producing a SFAS or an Interpretation. In response to the recommendation, the Board adopted the procedures described above. Under the prior policy, a TB was issued by the Staff, with little or no involvement by the Board and with little or no public comment.

As of September 1987, 42 Technical Bulletins had been issued. Examples include the following:

No. 79–7   Recoveries of a Previous Writedown under a Troubled Debt Restructuring Involving a Modification of Terms

---

[2]FASB Technical Bulletin 79-1 (revised), "Purpose and Scope of FASB Technical Bulletins and Procedures for Issuance," par. 4.

No. 81–2   Accounting for Unused Investment Tax Credits Acquired in a Business Combination Accounted for by the Purchase Method

No. 86–2   Accounting for an Interest in the Residual Value of a Leased Asset

It can be seen from the titles that the issues are narrow in scope compared to those addressed in other FASB pronouncements.

Other Publications

In addition to the four types of pronouncements described above, the FASB also publishes a number of other documents as part of its due process procedures and its public relations activities. These procedures and activities are described and discussed in the rest of this chapter.

THE STEPS IN THE OVERALL PROCESS

The diversity of problems facing the FASB makes it impossible for identical due process procedures to be carried out for each project; nonetheless, similar steps must be applied for most individual projects in order to achieve the goals of the process.

The basic process is shown in the flowchart in Exhibit 3–1, which shows that up to six steps can take place. More information on each phase is provided in Exhibit 3–2, and this section of the chapter examines them in more detail.

Preliminary Evaluation of the Problem

A common question addressed to FASB Members and Staff members concerns the procedures for uncovering the problems the Board attempts to solve. The answer is not easily given because there are many ways in which the problems come to the FASB's attention.

One source is the **Emerging Issues Task Force** that was formed in 1984 to deal quickly with new problems. If the Task Force can reach a consensus about the solution to a narrow problem, no further action is taken. On the other hand, if the Task Force reaches a consensus that a problem is important and agrees that its solution is unclear, it will recommend that the Board undertake the development of a more careful resolution of the issues.

As described in Chapter 2, another formal source of issues is **FASAC**, which also advises on the priority of problems. Through the work of the Agenda Advisory Committee, the Council can encourage the Board to undertake a new project.

A key duty of the Research and Technical Activities Staff is to closely monitor the newspapers and periodicals in the **business press** for stories

EXHIBIT 3–1 Steps in the FASB's Due Process

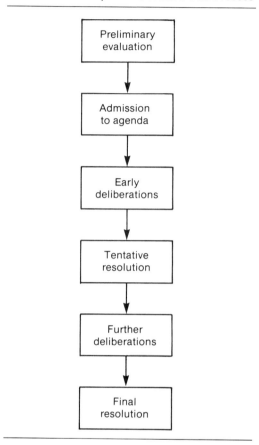

about unusual transactions, events, or conditions that create financial accounting issues. When one of these things does occur, a Staff member may make preliminary inquiries to determine the details and the potential for its occurrence in other settings. If it appears that the problem could be pervasive, the Staff will begin to work toward determining whether the Board should add a project to its agenda.

Another task of the Staff is responding to **technical inquiries** received from preparers and auditors by telephone and in writing. Although many of these inquiries can be handled on an ad hoc basis, some may lead to the development of a Technical Bulletin or another type of pronouncement.

EXHIBIT 3-2   Summary of the FASB's Due Process

Step	Activity	Possible Publications
1. Preliminary evaluation of problem	Emerging Issues Task Force Agenda Advisory Committee of FASAC Monitoring press Constituent communications SEC recommendation	Research studies
2. Admission to agenda	Board meetings	None
3. Early deliberations	Staff literature search Project Task Force Project Advisory Group Public hearings Board meetings	Discussion Memorandum Invitation to Comment
4. Tentative resolution	Board meetings Balloting	Tentative Conclusions Preliminary Views Exposure Draft
5. Further deliberations	Board meetings Public hearings	Revised Exposure Draft
6. Final resolution	Board meetings Balloting	Statements Interpretations

The Board also remains in communication with **professional groups**, such as the AICPA and the FEI, and is thus informed of emerging problems reported by their members. One particularly notable source of this kind is the AICPA's Accounting Standards Executive Committee (AcSEC).

In maintaining the relationship of "mutual nonsurprise" described in Chapter 1, the Board and the Staff communicate frequently with the **Securities and Exchange Commission and its staff**. Because the SEC staff examines the financial statements included with filings from all large companies, it is quickly informed about new problems. If the SEC's Chief Accountant and staff members cannot resolve a problem using the existing authoritative literature, they may suggest to the FASB that it conduct a study of the issues. For example, the SEC placed a moratorium on the capitalization of software development costs in 1983 and strongly encouraged the FASB to undertake a project to establish a standard in this area.

Occasionally, the FASB will seek to learn more about a problem before pursuing the possibility of putting it on the agenda as a project; in doing so, the FASB may commission a **Research Study** to examine it in detail. Studies are also executed at other stages in the process.

With respect to the **Defeasance** project, the Board became aware of the problem through the article in the July 7, 1982, *Wall Street Journal* that appears on page 2 in the Prologue. The person who first noticed the article was then Chairman Don Kirk, who instructed J. T. Ball to have someone look into the transactions and into the authoritative literature that might apply to them. Within a matter of a few weeks, the project was under way.

Admission to the Agenda

The mere discovery of a problem is not sufficient to assure that the FASB will undertake its solution. Other conditions must exist, and the Board must agree to admit the problem to the agenda. In doing so, it deliberates the question in one or more public meetings, following the usual meeting process described on page 67.

A decision by the Board to create an agenda project not only commits its own resources but also mobilizes the business community by inviting its participation in the due process procedures. As a consequence of this involvement, substantial deliberation takes place before this decision is made. A number of factors must enter into the decision. The following three points are always considered:

- The problem must be **sufficiently significant** in terms of its effect on the financial statements and its pervasiveness throughout the economy—if the problem does not create significant difficulties, the cost of the due process may not be justifiable.

- The alternative solutions to the problem must be sufficiently different to be **controversial**—if there is no serious disagreement about the answer (or no significant difference in the financial statements from applying the alternatives), an authoritative resolution is not necessary.
- There must be a suitably **high likelihood that the Board can resolve the issues** in a manner that will be acceptable to the constituency—without some prior sense of the likelihood that the Board Members will be able to reach a consensus, it is generally not advisable to undertake a formal project.

If the Board cannot determine whether a particular problem merits a project, it often instructs the Staff to carry out further study rather than completely rejecting the possibility of creating a project.

One important dimension of the agenda decision is the determination of what type of pronouncement would be issued at the completion of the project. For the big issues related to the Conceptual Framework, there was simply no debate—a Statement of Financial Accounting Concepts was needed. In other specific situations, it is clear that a Statement of Financial Accounting Standards is needed because the transactions, events, or conditions to be accounted for have not occurred or existed before or have not been addressed in the authoritative literature. In less certain situations, the decision may be made to issue a SFAS in order to assure that the due process procedures are complete, even though another type of pronouncement may eventually emerge. Only when a problem is narrow or similar to others that have been previously resolved will the Board decide to issue an Interpretation or Technical Bulletin.

Concerning the **Defeasance** project, information coming to the Board from the SEC, auditors, and many other members of the business community clearly indicated that the new kind of transaction had created an important financial accounting problem. Although similar transactions had occurred for tax-exempt debt, the Board did not believe that the solution applied in those situations was readily transferable to the transactions that had occurred or that were likely to occur. Additionally, there were significantly different positions on how to account for the transaction. As described in the August 13, 1982, *Wall Street Journal* article on page 4 in the Prologue, some wanted to recognize a gain on the income statement and eliminate the debt from the statement of financial position, while others disagreed. Finally, the Board Members determined that a resolution was likely because a majority of them initially thought that a gain probably should not be recognized (the August 9, 1982, article from *Corporate Financing Week* reports this fact). In order to assure that the problem received full and careful consideration, with participation from all parts of the business community, the Board decided to pursue the development of a new standard instead of merely trying to develop an Interpretation of APB Opinion 26 or SFAS 4, both of which concern early extinguishment of debt.

Financial Accounting Standards Board Meeting Room.

FASB MEETING PROCEDURES

Frequency. Typically, the Board meets on Wednesday of each week in its meeting room in the Stamford headquarters.

Announcement. Each meeting is announced in a weekly newsletter called *Action Alert*. The announcement briefly describes the specific issues to be discussed for each project that has been scheduled.

Public attendance. The general public is admitted to the meeting up to the seating capacity of the room, which is determined by local ordinances to be only 66 persons, including the Board and Staff members. Typically, the number attending is much smaller than the capacity. The audience is not allowed to participate in the discussion, although (on rare occasions) a specific person may be called on by the Chairman to illuminate a particular point. Copies of the documents being discussed by the Board and Staff members are not available to the public as a matter of economy and to prevent preliminary positions from being perceived as final. Consequently, the discussion is occasionally difficult for the audience to follow. The audience usually includes representatives of public accounting firms, the SEC, and others especially interested in the particular issues under consideration.

Preliminary sessions. At least one week before each meeting, the Staff gives Board Members memorandums that identify the specific issues and other questions that are to be addressed and resolved in the public meeting. Then (usually on Monday and Tuesday), the project team holds private meetings with all Board Members (in groups of one, two, or three) to gauge their reactions and understand their preliminary positions, as well as to brief them on the thoughts of the other Board Members.

The meeting. When the Board meeting actually begins, a Staff member summarizes the points under consideraton, primarily for the benefit of the audience. The ensuing discussion usually repeats the results of the preliminary meetings, although the dynamics of the session may generate movement toward a consensus.

Minutes. No transcripts or other detailed minutes are prepared for the meeting; rather, the Staff members involved in the project are responsible for preparing an unpublished summary document which is available to the public for examination and duplication. A shorter summary (only a few sentences in length) is published in the *Action Alert* printed during the following week.

Early Deliberations

To the extent that it was not done in the prior stages, the creation of an agenda project triggers Staff effort toward more carefully identifying the underlying issues and the alternative positions on them. This phase generally includes a review of the authoritative and other professional literature on the topic, and may produce additional research studies. The Staff may also conduct surveys of statement users and other groups to define the nature and extent of the problem.

In some situations, the Staff will make its contact with the constituencies more formal by creating a **Task Force** or an **Advisory Group** composed of individuals whose experiences have provided them with special insights on the issues. For major projects, the Staff forms a Task Force that typically has about 20 members (some have as few as 10 and others as many as 30). For Implementation and Practice Problem projects, a smaller Advisory Group may be created, typically with 6 to 10 members. In some cases, the Advisory Group may actually be formed in the agenda decision phase to assist the Staff in making its recommendation to the Board. Many projects do not have any formal groups; in these cases, the Project Manager merely maintains contact with a few knowledgeable people.

In some major projects (but certainly not all), the Task Force will assist the Staff in publishing a **discussion document** that solicits responses from the constituencies to help identify the important issues and to help assess the merits of the different positions on previously identified issues. The document may be called a **Discussion Memorandum** (DM) or an **Invitation to Comment** (ITC). A DM is typically drafted entirely by the Staff and is fairly broad in its scope. An ITC is often partially drafted by those other than the Staff and is more narrowly focused. After the document has been published, the Task Force or Advisory Group may have no further official function; however, the Project Manager may keep it intact so that he or she can call on some or all of its members for advice as the due process continues. Members are also encouraged to remain actively involved in later phases of the process.

When the project is sufficiently significant, or when the Board Members want to become more completely informed, the Staff will arrange a round of **public hearings** subsequent to the publication of the discussion document. Through announcements in **Action Alert** and in the discussion document itself, as well as by other means, potential respondents are invited to present their views to the Board and Staff. Those who wish to present their positions at the hearing must first submit a written comment so that Board Members can get the most out of the process. After a brief oral testimony, the participants then respond to questions from the Members. A hearing may last only one day, or it may go on for longer periods. For example, four rounds of public hearings on the Pension project took more than ten days to complete. Altogether, 175 presentations were made.

Throughout this early stage in the due process, the responses to the discussion documents are analyzed by the Staff and sent to the Board Members together with summaries. The issues are also discussed at Board meetings, and in private sessions between the Staff and individual Board Members. No formal votes are compiled, although a straw poll may be taken to establish the extent of the consensus on particular questions. Of course, the Staff project team develops an idea of Board Members' positions through the course of the deliberations.

For the **Defeasance** project, it was determined that the urgency of solving the problem necessitated limiting the due process steps. Thus, neither a Task Force nor an Advisory Group was created, no discussion document was published, and no public hearings were convened. Instead, Bob Wilkins, the Project Manager, developed an informal network of contacts in public accounting, banking, corporate finance, and the government to gain a sense of the constituencies' positions on the issues. Through the steps described in the next section, sufficient opportunity was available to all members of the business community to make their views known to the FASB.

Tentative Resolution

After the early deliberations are completed, the Board moves on to the next stage of the due process, which involves a more formal description of the Members' positions on the issues and any consensus that may have developed. Although abstract discussions are informative, they do not generate the public interest that a concrete proposal can create. To focus this interest and to "test the waters," as well as to solicit responses from constituency members who have not participated in the earlier stages, the Board publishes documents that describe a proposed solution to the problem.

For two especially complex and controversial projects, the Board issued special documents that outlined its position. In 1976, it issued a **Tentative Conclusions** document on the Conceptual Framework project as part of a Discussion Memorandum. In 1982, it issued a **Preliminary Views** document on the Pensions project.

An **Exposure Draft** *must* be published for all projects that lead to a Statement of Financial Accounting Standards or a Statement of Financial Accounting Concepts. A Draft *may* be published for an Interpretation, but not necessarily. This document is essentially a *pro forma* final document, including a discussion of the problem, a presentation of the proposed solution, a proposed effective date, and a discussion of the reasons underlying the Board's decision. It is published only if a majority of the Board Members vote for its publication. Board Members who do not agree with the majority can cause the draft to include their "alternative views," but their names are not identified. Of course, to those who have followed the project closely, the identity of the dissenters is quite obvious.

The first Exposure Draft for the **Defeasance** project was published in October 1982. Its proposed solution confirmed the initial tentative decision to not allow gains to be recognized on the income statement. However, it proposed that the debtor reduce the carrying value of the debt by subtracting the market value of the assets in the trust; the remaining credit balance would be left on the statement of financial position in the liability section. Approximately 41,000 copies of the Exposure Draft were mailed, but only 62 responses were received. According to the analysis compiled by the FASB staff, the responses came from the following groups: public accounting (13), industry (38), securities industry (3), banking (5), academe (1), government (1), and law (1). Most of the comment letters expressed dissatisfaction with the proposed solution.

Further Deliberations

Following the return and analysis of the responses to the Exposure Draft, the Board again discusses the issues to determine if any evidence has been uncovered that has led to the reversal of a Member's previous position. In rare circumstances, more public hearings may be held. For example, hearings were held in the Winter of 1987 subsequent to the issuance of the Exposure Draft on accounting for income taxes.

There are three possible outcomes of this stage of the due process:

- The project may be terminated.
- Another Exposure Draft may be issued.
- The Board may move on to a final pronouncement.

A project will be terminated if the responses indicate that the problem is not significant or that the Board will be unable to resolve the problem in a way acceptable to the constituents, or if it appears that the Board will not be able to reach a consensus. This step has occurred only very rarely. For example, the Board decided in 1975 against issuing a standard based on an Exposure Draft calling for the disclosure of price-level-adjusted information, primarily because the SEC had established its own (and far different) requirements for accounting for changing prices. Another example was the Board's decision in 1982 not to press ahead with a final Concepts statement on reporting income, cash flows, and financial position because the responses to the Exposure Draft revealed substantial misgivings among the constituencies and because it became apparent that the Board Members were more divided on the issues than they had been when the draft was published. Some of the material in the Exposure Draft was finally included in SFAC 5, but it was only a small portion of the original.

Small changes can usually be incorporated into the final statement without difficulty or controversy; however a second Exposure Draft will be issued at this stage if a significantly different solution is preferred by a majority of the Board. Although this step of issuing a second draft has been taken more often than completely dropping a project, it is relatively uncommon.

Because of the opposing views expressed in the comment letters on the first Exposure Draft and as a result of the ensuing Board deliberations, a second Exposure Draft for the **Defeasance** project was issued in July 1983. Its requirements constituted a reversal of the initial position endorsed by the Board. Specifically, for investments meeting certain limiting criteria, the second draft proposed completely removing the liability and the invested assets from the statement of financial position and recognizing a gain on the income statement. This time, approximately 38,000 copies were distributed and 74 responses were received. According to the analysis compiled by the FASB staff, the 74 responses to this second Exposure Draft came from the following groups: public accounting (15), industry (47), securities industry (3), banking (7), academe (1), and government (1). This distribution is essentially the same as the first, except that two more responses were received from the public accounting profession and the banking industry, while nine more came from statement preparers. Like the situation seen for the sources of the FASB's contributions, the large proportion of responses from preparers and the small proportion from users are potentially a matter of serious concern. The Epilogue discusses this potential problem in detail.

Final Resolution

After further discussions among Board Members in small groups and public meetings, the Staff prepares an internal "Ballot Draft" of the final pronouncement for distribution to the Board. If a majority votes for its approval, it is published as a Statement or Interpretation. Those members who voted against its issuance are identified, and the nature of their dissent is described in the document.

For the **Defeasance** project, the Board issued SFAS 76 in November 1983, with some minor revisions of the requirements proposed in the second Exposure Draft. There were four assenting votes and three dissents. This quotation is illustrative of the content and style of a dissent.

> Messrs. Kirk, March, and Mosso dissent from this Statement because they do not believe that extinguishment of debt accounting and resultant gain or loss recognition should be extended to situations wherein the "debtor is not legally released from being the primary obligor under the debt obligation." . . . In their opinion, the setting aside of assets in trust does not, in and of itself, constitute either the disposition of assets with potential gain or loss recognition or the satisfaction of a liability with potential gain or loss recognition. . . . Dedicating the assets might ensure that the debt is serviced in timely fashion, but that event alone just matches up cash flows; it does not satisfy, eliminate, or extinguish the obligation. For a debt to be satisfied, the creditor must be satisfied.

On one occasion, the Board decided to issue a final pronouncement in a form different from the one that was originally contemplated. This action occurred when the responses to a 1982 Exposure Draft of a standard on accounting for the investment tax credit indicated that the problem was too narrow to justify issuing a statement. Consequently, the final decision was to issue Technical Bulletin 83–1, "Accounting for the Reduction in the Tax Basis of an Asset Caused by the Investment Tax Credit."

Subsequent Review

The due process procedures do not always stop after the issuance of the final pronouncement, particularly for controversial projects. The Board attempts to monitor the acceptance of a pronouncement *informally* through communications with the constituents, in much the same way that it attempts to locate new problems. On occasion, the Board has also *formally* solicited comments from its constituents concerning standards that are in place. Additionally, one function of FASAC members is to report to the Board any problems that have been created or left unsolved by a pronouncement.

As a result of these processes, the Board may decide to issue a Technical Bulletin or an Interpretation to resolve a minor problem. In other cases, an additional Standard may be needed to expand the applicability of the earlier solution or to solve a related problem that was not addressed in the initial document. As an extreme example, the Board found that SFAS 13 on accounting for leases needed to be supplemented by a series of later Standards, Interpretations, and Technical Bulletins to deal with a number of related problems (included are SFAS 17, 22, 23, 26, 27, 28, and 29, as well as Interpretations 19, 21, 23, 24, 26, and 27; and Technical Bulletins 79–10, 79–11, 79–12, 79–13, 79–14, 79–15, 79–16, 79–17, 79–18, 85–3, and 86–2).

In a few cases, the Board has issued a subsequent pronouncement that drastically altered an earlier one. For example, SFAS 25 (on oil and gas accounting) was issued to indicate that the requirements of SFAS 19 were not to be imposed; it was needed because the SEC did not accept the solution provided in SFAS 19. SFAS 52 (on translation of foreign currency) was issued to replace SFAS 8, which proved extremely unpopular among financial statement preparers. SFAS 82 and SFAS 89 were issued to rescind the disclosures of SFAS 33 because their continued use was not supported by research, the Board Members, or the constituencies.

For the **Defeasance** project, Technical Bulletin 84–4 was issued in October 1984 to deal with "Instantaneous In-Substance Defeasance," in which companies were borrowing funds, immediately investing them in securities acquired in a different market (often in another country), and recognizing a gain. The TB excluded such arrangements from the basic treatment established in SFAS 76.

PUBLIC RELATIONS ACTIVITIES

In addition to all the preceding due process procedures, the FASB communicates with the business world in other ways because it is sensitive to its role as the focal point of a political process. On the basis that a better informed constituency is more likely to participate in the due process, support specific pronouncements, and provide financial support, the Board carries on a number of **public relations** activities, which are coordinated through Mr. Robert Van Riper, a full-time Public Relations Counsel. These activities include the publication of several newsletters.

Action Alert was mentioned earlier. This weekly summary of future and recent Board meetings is distributed to between 1,500 and 2,000 subscribers.

Status Report is issued irregularly, but about 15 issues are published each year. It describes other events relating to the Board, and summarizes new and proposed pronouncements. The first issue of each quarter includes the "Technical Plan," which describes the status of each project on the agenda and the schedule of expected events, such as the publication of an Exposure Draft or the convening of a public hearing. *Status Report* is distributed to approximately 66,000 subscribers.

Viewpoints provides a forum for the expression of unofficial or personal opinions of Board and Staff members, and others. It has been used to report the results of research projects that are not published as separate Research Studies and to obtain wider circulation of speeches. It is distributed to subscribers of *Status Report.*

The Public Relations Office also prepares an annual version of *Facts about FASB* for free distribution to any interested individuals or groups. This publication includes a "mission statement" for the Board and short biographies of the Board Members, and the Director and Assistant Director of the Research and Technical Activities Staff. Approximately 100,000 copies are printed and distributed each year.[3] A shorter version of *Facts about FASB* is prepared to describe the relationship between the Board and the federal government. It is also available without charge, but is not as widely distributed as the more complete version.

The FASB has sponsored several special conferences on significant and controversial topics. Their purpose is to provide a forum for the discussion of the issues and evidence relating to their solutions without the political (and possibly confrontational) nature of a public hearing or a Board meeting. For example, the Board has sponsored conferences on the Conceptual Framework, the economic consequences of accounting standards, and research related to accounting for changing prices.

In addition, Board Members, the Director of RTA, and Staff members

---

[3]In response to requests, *Facts about FASB* can be mailed out to accounting instructors for distribution to their classes.

are encouraged to accept speaking engagements in which they can explain the activities of the Board and receive comments and questions from significant constituent bodies. Thus, many speeches are delivered to major professional groups in national, regional, and local meetings. They are also given to college and university groups, including Beta Alpha Psi chapters and student accounting clubs. In 1986, 169 speeches were presented; 65 of these were delivered by Board Members, 23 by the Director of RTA, and 81 by members of the Staff and others.

The Board also maintains an ongoing relationship with the press, particularly with publications that focus on business affairs. To help assure that reporters have access to accurate explanations of all new pronouncements, press releases are distributed to about 500 major newspapers and other periodicals. In special circumstances, news conferences are held to allow reporters to obtain clarification from Board and Staff members. Press conferences have been held on such occasions as the release of the Exposure Draft on foreign currency translation (eventually issued as SFAS 52) and the publication of the Board's Preliminary Views on pensions. In other cases, special "Background Briefings" have been provided in Washington for government personnel, and the press was invited to attend and participate. Three such meetings were held in 1983 concerning the projects on Pensions and Income Taxes.

In dealing with the FASB, press representatives generally do not seek interviews with Board Members for their positions on issues; instead, they usually prefer to deal with the Project Manager. Although this practice of contacting Project Managers is not the result of a deliberate policy, it is useful to the Board because it allows Board Members more flexibility in changing from a preliminary position on the issues. For example, if the press had quoted a specific Member as being against the recognition of a defeasance gain, it would have been more difficult for him to change to the opposite position, regardless of how persuasive the arguments were.

PARTICIPATING IN THE FASB'S DUE PROCESS PROCEDURES

It may be apparent from the preceding discussion that the nature and contents of FASB pronouncements are shaped at least in part by communications from the Board's constituents. This section is provided for the guidance of those readers who would like to affect the outcome of the process by participating directly in it.

In interviews with the authors, Board and key Staff members asserted that comment letters and testimony at public hearings do indeed affect their positions on the issues. However, they also agreed that all communications are not equally effective in accomplishing the senders' goals. To help readers understand more about the process and participate in it more effectively, the authors asked Board and Staff members to identify the qualities of effective and ineffective communications. Some of those comments are presented below:

- Articulate, well-presented arguments are effective. Presentations that dismiss opposing views out of hand as simply wrong or "stupid" are especially ineffective.
- Effective communications are neither too long nor too short. Letters with many single-spaced pages are likely to be overlooked because the writer does not focus on the critical points. On the other hand, very short letters merely demonstrate that the respondents do not understand the controversies.
- Responses that include clear examples are well received, especially if they provide insight into the effects of a proposed treatment on common transactions in a nonmainstream industry (such as software development).
- In general, letters that merely promote the respondent's self-interest are not considered effective. One Board Member said that he finds such letters to be interesting, but asserted that they are helpful only if the respondents clearly know that their position is self-serving and do not try to stretch logic beyond its limits.
- Comment letters are not used to "count noses" on the popularity of a preliminary position. Accordingly, multiple copies of the same letter from different members of the same constituency are particularly ineffective. One Board Member said that he seldom finds such letter-writing "campaigns" to be convincing but he does consider them useful for gauging how deeply the issues affect respondents' emotions.
- Threatening letters are especially ineffective.

One Board Member said that presentations at public hearings varied significantly in their effectiveness. He pointed out that presentations that follow up on a previously submitted comment letter are particularly useful. He also indicated that interesting and lively presentations are more likely to get points across whereas presentations read from prepared scripts are "duds." Finally, he cautioned that arrogance or overaggressiveness is likely to be counterproductive.

APPENDIX
Obtaining FASB Publications

To participate effectively in the FASB's due process procedures, respondents must be well informed on the issues and the preliminary deliberations that have taken place prior to the Board's solicitation of comments. To be informed, the respondents need to have access to facts about what has already happened. Although public accounting firms and other organizations publish summaries (such as those contained in *DH + S Review,* distributed by Deloitte Haskins & Sells), they are seldom as complete or as timely as the materials provided by the FASB to those who subscribe to its publications. The following subscription packages were available in 1987:

- The **Comprehensive Plan** includes all publications of the FASB, except for *Action Alert;* its cost is $125 for one year or $230 for two years. A 20 percent discount applies to all educators and to Associate Members who donate at least $200 to the Financial Accounting Foundation.
- The **Basic Plan** includes only final documents (and thus omits Exposure Drafts and Discussion Memoranda) and *Status Report;* its cost is $60 for 12 months or $110 for 24 months, with the same 20 percent discount to Associate Members and educators.
- *Action Alert* is distributed only by separate subscription, which costs $36 per year; no discounts are offered.

Single copies of Discussion Memoranda and Exposure Drafts are available without charge during the comment period. Multiple copies of these documents and any copies of final pronouncements must be purchased through the Board's Publications Office. The Board also markets volumes that combine the pronouncements of the Committee on Accounting Procedure, the Accounting Principles Board, and the FASB. The *Original Pronouncements* volume presents the material in chronological order and indicates which sections have been amended or superseded; the *Current Text* volume takes the material out of the original format and recombines it by subject matter for easier reference when dealing with a specific topic, such as executive compensation or treasury stock.

For additional information or to order materials, inquiry should be addressed to:

> Publications Office
> Financial Accounting Standards Board
> High Ridge Park
> P.O. Box 3821
> Stamford, Connecticut 06903-0821

SELECTED READINGS

KELLY-NEWTON, LAUREN. *Accounting Policy Formulation: The Role of Corporate Management.* Reading, Mass.: Addison-Wesley Publishing, 1980.

KIRK, DONALD J. "Concepts, Consensus, and Compromise: Their Roles in Standard Setting." *Journal of Accountancy,* April 1981, pp. 83–86.

NAKAYAMA, M.; S. LIEBEN; and M. BENIS. "Due Process and FASB No. 13." *Management Accounting,* April 1981, pp. 49–53.

REVIEW QUESTIONS

1. What is the meaning of the term *due process?*
2. What are the five broad goals of the FASB's due process procedures?
3. Why is due process considered essential by the FASB?
4. Identify the four types of final pronouncements issued by the FASB.
5. What actions unambiguously designate Statements of Financial Accounting Standards as generally accepted accounting principles?
6. What document must precede all final SFASs?
7. How many Board Members must vote in favor of a standard before it can be issued?
8. Are FASB Interpretations part of GAAP, and if so, what is the source of their authority?
9. Discuss the purpose of an FASB Interpretation.
10. Compare the due process steps for an SFAS with the due process steps for an Interpretation.
11. How many Board Members must vote in favor of an Interpretation before it can be issued?
12. Do Statements of Financial Accounting Concepts create GAAP? Why or why not?
13. What are the purposes of a Statement of Financial Accounting Concepts?
14. What due process procedures were followed in the development of SFACs?
15. Identify the topics of the six SFACs.
16. Do Technical Bulletins create GAAP?
17. What is the purpose of a Technical Bulletin?
18. Identify the circumstances that lead to the issuance of a Technical Bulletin.
19. Discuss the due process followed for the development of a Technical Bulletin.
20. Identify the six basic steps that might be taken in the due process for an FASB project.
21. Discuss some of the ways used to uncover the problems that the Board attempts to solve.
22. Discuss the three factors that the Board always considers when deciding whether to add a project to its agenda.
23. What are some activities that might take place during the early deliberations stage of the Board's due process?
24. What documents might be published in the tentative resolution stage of the due process?

25. After the analysis of responses to an Exposure Draft and further discussions by the Board, what are the three possible outcomes of the further deliberations stage of the due process?

26. What circumstances would cause a project to be terminated after an Exposure Draft has been issued?

27. What are the activities in the final resolution stage of the due process?

28. Briefly identify the activities that might take place in the subsequent review stage of the due process.

29. Why is the public relations function a useful part of the FASB's operations?

30. Identify the newsletters published by the FASB.

31. Identify FASB public relations publications or activities other than newsletters.

32. Identify some of the characteristics of effective communication with the FASB.

EXERCISES

1. You are the chief financial officer of a major corporation. The FASB has recently released an Exposure Draft that would cause the earnings of your corporation to plummet if it becomes a standard. What avenues would you use to respond to the FASB? Would your answer change if your corporation's earnings were expected to rise sharply as a result of the standard?

2. Obtain a copy of a Discussion Memorandum or an Exposure Draft, and prepare a comment letter. It is important that you attempt to incorporate the characteristics of an effective comment letter that were described by Board and Staff Members. Your instructor will indicate whether your should use a specific document or one that you select.

3. Several general steps are included in the due process followed by the FASB for establishing accounting standards. This process is followed to assure that the interests of the FASB's constituents have been considered.

    a. What were the major due process steps associated with the establishment of SFAS 34, "Capitalization of Interest Costs," issued in October 1979?

    b. What were the major due process steps associated with the establishment of SFAS 33, "Financial Reporting and Changing Prices," issued in September 1979?

    c. Compare the due process steps used in SFAS 34 and SFAS 33.

4. Following are four actual letters that the FASB received in response to two exposure drafts.

    a. Identify the basic position taken by each respondent. Do you agree or disagree with the position? Is there sufficient support for the argument that is presented? Did the writer use the Conceptual Framework? If so, was it used well? What is the overall effectiveness of each comment letter?

    b. Select one comment letter and suggest how any deficiencies in its arguments or presentation could be corrected. You should not suggest a change in the basic position for or against the Board's proposal.

December 15, 1982

Director of Research and Technical Activities, File Reference No. 1032
Financial Accounting Standards Board
High Ridge Park
Stamford, Connecticut 06905

Gentlemen:

I seldom write to the Financial Accounting Standards Board on its pronounce-ments because experience has taught me that it is usually a useless exercise. However, the Board's preliminary views on accounting for pensions cry out for a response from every financial executive.

In all my years in the financial arena, I have never seen such an absolutely ridic-ulous proposal. This is the ultimate triumph of academia over common sense. Pension liability estimates are just that at best. The potential margin for error, particularly in plans with less than 1,000 or so participants, is very significant. To dignify these "actuarial" estimates by recording them as assets and liabilities would be virtually unthinkable except for the fact that the FASB has done equally stupid things in the past (FASB 8 says it all).

Should the present FASB thinking on this subject become the law of the land, we will refuse to recognize it and will encourage all of our peers to do likewise.

For God's sake, use common sense just this once.

Sincerely,

John E. Powers

February 8, 1985

Director of Research and Technical Activities
File Reference No. 1080-024
Financial Accounting Standards Board
High Ridge Park
P.O. Box 3821
Stamford, Connecticut 06905-0821

Members of the Financial Accounting Standards Board:

The Boeing Company is pleased to comment on the proposed Statement of Financial Accounting Standards—"Induced Conversions of Convertible Debt." The Company concurs with the Board's proposal to amend APB Opinion 26 to exclude transactions of this type. However, we believe that a conversion involving the issuance of additional shares as an inducement does not result in an "expense" to the enterprise and therefore disagree with the proposed accounting treatment.

Expenses are defined in SFAC No. 3 as: "...outflows or other using up of assets or incurrence of liabilities..." (para 65); which "...represent actual or expected cash outflows (or the equivalent) that have occurred or will eventuate..." (para 66). Accordingly, the issuance of previously unissued stock of a company does not result in expense since unissued stock is not recognized as an asset and no cash outflow has occurred or will eventuate as a result of the transaction. This is further supported by para 101(i) of the same statement: "stock dividends payable are not liabilities because they do not involve an obligation to make future sacrifices of assets." The mere issuance of stock (at whatever price) does not represent the consuming of assets. Any foregone gains on hypothetical open market stock sales should not be forced into the earnings statement.

The proper accounting for such a conversion, regardless of the number of shares issued, should be a reduction of debt for the amount converted and an equal credit to capital stock (which represents the amount actually contributed to the enterprise). In the event cash consideration is paid to induce conversion the amount should be treated as partial payment of the debt. Stock issued should be related to the remaining debt converted.

Although no expense would be recognized in the earnings statement from the issuance of incremental shares, the effect of such conversions on stockholders equity should of course be disclosed. The statement for "investments by and distributions to owners during the period" (as addressed in SFAC No. 5) would be the appropriate statement for recognizing transactions of this type.

In summary, the Company believes no expense should be recognized unless economic resources are or will be consumed or given up. Typically an increase in the number of shares issued in conversion does not alter the economic effect of the transaction on the enterprise either in terms of cost or benefit.

We appreciate the opportunity to provide our views on this matter for due consideration by the Board.

Very truly yours,

D. J. DeMers
Assistant Controller

February 1, 1985

Director of Research and Technical Activities
File Reference No. 1080-024
Financial Accounting Standards Board
High Ridge Park, P.O. Box 3821
Stamford, Connecticut 06905–0821

Dear Mr. Leisenring:

Pacific Telesis Group is pleased to respond to your request for comments to the proposed Statement of Financial Accounting Standards entitled *Induced Conversions of Convertible Debt.*

We do not endorse the Board's proposed amendment to APB No. 26. We do not feel the addition of an inducement changes the economic substance of a conversion transaction. We feel that all extinguishments of convertible debt instruments are fundamentally alike, and that any additional consideration to induce the debt holder to convert should be included in the gain or loss recognized at conversion, as is done today.

Additionally, we are concerned that the proposed amendment may have negative impact on rate-regulated utilities. Currently, the regulator may allow costs associated with extinguishment of debt to be recovered over a specified period. Under this proposed amendment, if an inducement is offered, the recognition of expenses would be limited to that expense equal to the fair value of only the additional assets or securities issued. This could seriously impair recovery of any unamortized interest or issuance costs.

In conclusion, we propose the Board make a comprehensive review of extinguishment of debt. The need for a comprehensive review is indicated by the amount of recent standard setting activity in this area.

Again, we express our appreciation for the opportunity to comment on this important proposal.

Sincerely,

F. V. Spiller
Vice President and Comptroller

March 7, 1985

Director of Research and Technical Activities
Financial Accounting Standards Board
High Ridge Park, P.O. Box 3821
Stamford, Connecticut 06905–0821

Re: File Reference No. 1080–024

Dear Sir:

Robert Morris Associates, as a financial information user group, appreciates the opportunity to respond to the exposure Draft on Induced Conversions of Convertible Debt.

We agree with the proposed conclusions in the draft that the debtor enterprise should recognize an expense equal to the fair value of the incremental consideration (the inducement) issued or paid. This type of transaction is separate and distinct from conversions or redemptions under the original convertible debt instrument. In our opinion, the transaction should definitely be reflected in the current income statement and not as a reduction of equity capital as one Board member proposes. If the amount is material, the transaction should be separately identified. This recommended accounting for the transaction is compatible with the accounting set forth in APB Opinion No. 26, "Early Extinguishment of Debt."

We also agree that the measurement date of the transaction should be the date the inducement offer is accepted by the convertible debt holder.

If you have further questions regarding our opinions, please contact us.

Very truly yours,

Patrick L. Flynn,
President

4

Some Recurring
Accounting Controversies

This chapter reviews several of the most significant and controversial financial accounting issues that have been raised over the last 50 to 75 years and tackled by authoritative standards-setting bodies, including the FASB. The survey demonstrates several points.

First, it shows that big issues seldom go away. They may appear in old familiar forms as different people gain power and want to bring them up for reconsideration. They also may appear in new forms when new types of transactions or other arrangements are developed. In either case, a resolution of an issue embodied in an authoritative pronouncement is seldom the end of the debate.

Second, it demonstrates the four implications of politics on GAAP that were drawn at the end of the first chapter. Specifically, it is argued there that politics make GAAP logically inconsistent, that someone will be unhappy with any resolution of an issue, and that GAAP *will* change, although the process of change will probably be slow and arduous.

Most important, perhaps, the review of the issues also demonstrates how **the people, the process, and the politics** of accounting standards setting have come together in the past, and will continue to come together in the future.

This chapter discusses the following issues:

Note: the authors express special appreciation to Dr. J. T. Ball, Assistant Director of Research and Technical Activities and Dr. Reed K. Storey, Senior Technical Advisor at the FASB, for their assistance in providing background material for this chapter.

☐ Capitalization versus expensing
- Research and development costs
- Interest costs
- Software development costs
- Oil and gas accounting

☐ Off-balance-sheet financing
- Leases
- Pensions
- Unconsolidated finance subsidiaries

☐ Income taxes
- Deferred taxes
- Investment tax credit

☐ Changing prices
- Price-level adjustments
- Current value

By the nature of this book, the discussions are not full presentations of all facets of the controversies or the alternative positions on the issues. However, they are sufficiently complete for the purposes at hand.

CAPITALIZATION VERSUS EXPENSING

The fundamental issue of capitalization versus expensing concerns the choice that arises after a cost has been incurred by giving up an asset, creating a liability, or creating owners' equity. Specifically, the question is whether the debit for the transaction should be recognized as an **asset** that will appear on the statement of financial position or as an **expense** that will appear on the income statement.

In general, preparers of financial statements tend to want to *capitalize* costs by placing them on the statement of financial position. This accounting keeps income higher, results in higher stockholders' equity, and improves the ratio of debt to equity on the right-hand side of the statement. Capitalization also tends to produce a more stable income because the expense is spread over a number of years instead of being recognized all at once. The main disadvantage to preparers of capitalizing costs is that performance measures based on rates of return are depressed in future periods because the numerator (income) is reduced by amortization and the denominators (assets or equity) are increased. Thus, different circumstances may produce different preferences.

On the other hand, auditors might tend to favor expensing all of the cost because doing so eliminates the risk that the statement of financial position would overstate an asset or even reflect an asset that really does not exist.

Users, in contrast, have no reason to prefer one method over the other as long as only real assets are capitalized and only real expenses are reported on the income statement.

It should be clear that this issue is very pervasive. It reaches into all areas of accounting and into many, many transactions. Most often, the issue is not controversial. For example, when the cost is incurred to purchase a physical asset or to pay managers' salaries, it is generally clear that the former is capitalized, while the latter is expensed.

In many other situations, however, the question of whether to capitalize or expense a cost is very controversial. The following discussion deals with four types of costs that have been persistently troublesome: research and development costs, interest costs, software development costs, and oil and gas accounting.

Research and Development Costs

The capitalization issue for research and development costs is made controversial by the large sums some industries spend and by the difficulty of telling whether the expenditures produce any benefit. There is little disagreement that future benefits (and hence assets) are often generated from research and development activity. However, identifying which part of the costs produces the assets is difficult. An additional complicating factor is the question of whether the financial accounting standard for these costs should be designed to promote the policy of encouraging the discovery of new knowledge to keep United States industry progressive and to make the national defense stronger.

In the 1950s, most organizations were conservative and expensed research and development costs in the period in which they were incurred. However, a few companies capitalized some or all of these costs. One such company was Convair, a division of General Dynamics Corporation, which produced aircraft for commercial transportation and had capitalized large sums of research and development costs by the early 1960s. After a number of years, General Dynamics decided to get out of the commercial aircraft industry, and the previously capitalized costs were recognized as an expense in a single year. This expense was the largest write-off of previously capitalized costs in the history of accounting up to that time, and was a major impetus to the Accounting Principles Board's decision to begin studying accounting for research and development costs in the early 1960s.

Although the APB did not resolve the issue, it sponsored and published Accounting Research Study 14, "Accounting for Research and Development Expenditures," just before it went out of existence in 1973. This study defined research and development costs and suggested which of those costs might be capitalized.

The FASB put accounting for research and development costs on its initial agenda as a follow-up to the work performed by the APB. The first Discussion Memorandum published by the FASB was on research and development cost issues. SFAS 2, "Accounting for Research and Development Costs," which appeared in October 1974, established as mandatory the common practice of expensing research and development costs.[1] The Board Members apparently arrived at this conclusion for a variety of reasons, not the least of which must have been the desire to avoid the virtually impossible task of developing criteria that would specify when and how much to capitalize and expense without opening loopholes to preparers who would want to manipulate their financial statements.

Interest Costs

Traditionally, interest incurred on debts was virtually always reported as an expense. As early as 1917, however, some accountants advocated the position that interest was as necessary for the acquisition of an asset as any other costs that were being capitalized, such as the purchase price and installation costs.

In contrast to most entities, many utility companies capitalized interest costs. The technique was popular among these companies because the amount of recognized assets serves as their "rate base." This number multiplied by an acceptable rate of return equals the amount of income that is allowable under the regulations that apply to the company. By increasing the rate base rather than reporting interest costs as an expense, the company increases the amount of allowable income. This inclination is constrained, of course, by the fact the decision to postpone interest expense increases income and thereby makes a rate increase seem less necessary.

In the 1960s and 1970s, more nonutility companies began to capitalize interest costs. In 1974, the Securities and Exchange Commission placed a moratorium on the capitalization of interest costs until the issue could be studied by the FASB. In 1979, SFAS 34 was issued after a 4–3 vote; it requires capitalization of some interest costs on assets that are either constructed for a company's own use or constructed as a discrete project for sale or lease to another entity. Interest cost incurred after the asset has been put into use is expensed.

Software Development Costs

With the growth of the computer industry, there has been a commensurate increase in the number of companies formed to develop and market software. Many of these companies are small and struggling for survival, with the result that the capital market tends to impose a risk penalty on them by demanding a higher rate of return from their securities.

Because these companies usually incur large costs for personal services and have very few tangible assets, their balance sheets appear weak. To strengthen this appearance, many of the companies want to capitalize their product development costs instead of expensing them. One drawback of this

---

[1]More detailed information about this and other authoritative documents referenced in this chapter is presented in a separate section on page 102.

practice is that until software has been sold, there is little dependable evidence of its value. Furthermore, the useful life of software is so short that by the time its value is proven, it may no longer exist.

As a result of the large increase in the number of software development projects in the 1970s and the ambiguity of SFAS 2 on the question of whether software costs meet the definition of research and development costs, the FASB issued Interpretation 6 in 1975. It allowed capitalization of costs incurred to develop software for use in administration or sales activities and costs incurred to buy or lease software from other companies. However, the costs of developing software to be used in research and development activities could not be capitalized. The Board was not able to definitively resolve the issues concerning the treatment of the costs of other types of software, and provided only general guidance that some could be capitalized and some could not.

The situation remained unsettled until 1983, when another round of growth created many new software marketing companies that attempted to register new securities with the SEC. The Commission's staff grew uneasy about the widespread use of capitalization and imposed a moratorium on any new adoptions of that approach pending the establishment of more definitive guidance from the FASB. In 1984, the Board issued an Exposure Draft that attempted to provide more rigorous tests for determining whether a particular type of expenditure should be capitalized or expensed. Substantial opposition to parts of the preliminary position was expressed in comment letters and in testimony at hearings conducted in 1985. SFAS 86 was issued in August of that year; it requires capitalization of only certain costs incurred after the marketability of software has been established. Although this practice will be required, it should be clear that the controversy will continue.

Oil and Gas Accounting

Oil and gas companies also face a capitalization versus expense problem with respect to the cost of the many "dry holes" drilled for every producing well.

One view is that the costs of dry holes should be expensed because these wells did not produce any assets. Thus, only the costs of successful wells would be capitalized and then amortized over their useful life. This accounting approach is known as "successful efforts." In contrast, another view holds that *all* drilling is necessary to find good wells. The argument is made, therefore, that the costs of all wells should be capitalized, even those incurred in drilling dry holes. This accounting approach is known as "full costing."

The issue of how to account for oil and gas costs had been of low priority until the mid-1960s. However, an APB committee raised the issue because many of the smaller oil companies had adopted the full-cost method, whereas many large oil companies used the successful efforts method.

Because the oil and gas industry and the Big Eight auditing firms were divided on the question, the APB could not issue an opinion. The project was not included on the FASB's agenda; instead, the issue came to the top of Congress's list of priorities in the mid-1970s, when efforts were being made to develop a national policy to assure adequate supplies of energy. One facet of that policy was the restriction of the profits of energy producers, which in turn demanded satisfactory measures of profits. At that point, the diversity of practice for accounting for oil and gas costs became a stumbling block, and the Securities and Exchange Commission was instructed to develop an appropriate solution. Accordingly, the SEC turned to the FASB, which undertook an effort to settle the controversy.

The outcome was SFAS 19, "Financial Accounting and Reporting by Oil and Gas Producing Companies," which was issued in 1977. The successful efforts approach was selected over much opposition from smaller oil and gas companies, but with support from larger ones and most of the Big Eight. The SEC, conscious of its own constituencies, rejected SFAS 19 in 1978 with ASR 253, 257, and 259, and allowed both the successful efforts and full-cost methods to be used. The SEC then proposed "reserve recognition accounting" (RRA), which would recognize income when oil is discovered and when oil prices are increased rather than waiting until the oil is produced.

Thus, the SEC was able to avoid the troublesome capitalization versus expense controversy only by discarding traditional accounting concepts. Under RRA, all drilling costs would be deducted from income in the year they were incurred. Accordingly, a company that did not discover any oil or gas would not recognize an asset on the statement of financial position and would report a loss on the income statement. On the other hand, if the company were successful, it would show an asset equal to the value of the oil that was discovered and the income statement would reflect income equal to the difference between the value of the discovered resources and the costs incurred in finding them. The SEC's original proposal in 1978 was that RRA would be used only in supplemental disclosures for several years but would then become the primary basis of reporting. The proposal met opposition from the industry and auditors. Their arguments generally stated that there were no feasible methods of reliably determining the value of reserves. The SEC dropped its plans in 1981 not only because of these arguments but also because the newly elected Reagan administration was committed to deregulation and because public interest in the development of an energy policy was waning.

Because SFAS 19 was rejected by the SEC, it was substantially rescinded by SFAS 25, with the result that both full costing and successful efforts are still acceptable. When the SEC dropped its plans to make RRA mandatory, it encouraged the FASB to develop a standard to provide supplemental information similar to what would be produced by RRA. The Board completed this project in 1982 with the issuance of SFAS 69.

Another round in this controversy occurred in October 1986, when the SEC rejected a proposal from its Chief Accountant that successful efforts be established as the only acceptable method. Thus, it appears that the capitalization versus expensing issue will remain unresolved in this industry.

OFF-BALANCE-SHEET FINANCING

Other pervasive issues have arisen over the acceptability of practices that, in effect, allow a corporation to borrow money yet not recognize a liability on the statement of financial position. The nominal advantages to corporations of so-called off-balance-sheet financing practices are readily apparent. Because no liability is recorded, the company appears to be more solvent than it really is. On one hand, creditors and stockholders do not become alarmed by diminished solvency, and no unusual risk penalties are imposed on the company through a higher cost of capital. On the other hand, the omission is obvious to sophisticated users. Thus, it can be argued that the prices of the securities issued by these companies already reflect the effects of the higher risk.

Because of this benefit (however spurious it might appear), there have been numerous efforts to set up financing arrangements that allow a company to avoid putting debt on its balance sheet. This discussion considers three situations: leases, pensions, and unconsolidated finance subsidiaries.

Leases

A lease is an agreement whereby the owner of an asset allows another party to use it in exchange for a rental fee. For a simple lease, the arrangement is entered into for the convenience of the user, who in this way can avoid buying an asset that is used only infrequently or temporarily. Accounting for such simple leases is straightforward—the user (called the *lessee*) does not recognize an asset or liability on the balance sheet and reports only rent expense on the income statement.

The acceptability of such practices created an opportunity for off-balance-sheet financing to take place. By leasing an asset that would ordinarily be purchased, the lessee would not recognize either the asset or the debt. However, by making the lease cover a longer term, the lessee becomes the de facto owner of the asset, while the legal owner of the asset (called the *lessor*) merely serves as a secured lender.

In October 1949, the Committee on Accounting Procedures released ARB 38, which later became Chapter 14 of ARB 43. It required the footnotes of the lessee's financial statements to include descriptions of the amounts and timing of the annual payments to be paid and any other important terms of leases. These requirements were established in response to a growing number of "sale-and-leaseback" transactions in which a company built an asset, sold it to another company, and then immediately leased it back. In economic substance, the seller-lessee has borrowed the so-called selling price from the buyer-lessor, and the nominal rentals are nothing more than payments on the loan. Furthermore, the property has not been surrendered to the buyer, but has only been pledged as collateral against the loan. However, by applying acceptable practices, the asset was removed from the balance sheet, no liability was recognized, and rent expense was reported instead of depreciation and interest expense.

The Committee on Accounting Procedures had been studying accounting for leases when it was disbanded in 1959, and the APB decided to continue working on the project. The APB recognized its importance and made the topic one of the first five to be studied by the AICPA's newly created Accounting Research Division. The outcome was Accounting Research Study No. 4, "Reporting of Leases in Financial Statements," which was issued in 1962. Between 1962 and 1973, the APB issued four opinions (Nos. 5, 7, 27, and 31) dealing with leases. These four opinions essentially continued the same footnote requirements that had been established in ARB 38. Although Opinion 7 called for the capitalization of some leases, the APB was not able to generate a sufficient consensus to develop a more rigorous set of criteria that would significantly increase the number of lease agreements being reported on lessees' statements of financial position.

In the 1970s, the SEC got involved in accounting for leases because it appeared that the APB had not done enough to curb the excesses. Opinion 31, "Disclosure of Lease Commitments by Lessees," was a stopgap, last-gasp effort by the APB in response to concerns of the SEC.[2] In October 1973, the SEC issued Accounting Series Releases Nos. 132, 141, and 147, which required disclosures similar to those in APB Opinion 31 as well as additional mandatory footnote disclosures of the present value of certain lease commitments and the impact on net income that would have occurred if the company had capitalized leases that were in substance purchases of assets.

Despite the existence of one Accounting Research Bulletin, one Accounting Research Study, four APB Opinions, and three SEC Accounting Series Releases, many inconsistencies remained in lease accounting practices. Consequently, the FASB placed accounting for leases on its agenda. The FASB issued a Discussion Memorandum in July 1974 and held public hearings in November 1974. The Board received 306 responses to the Discussion Memorandum, and 32 presentations were made at the public hearings. The Board issued an Exposure Draft in August 1975, and received 250 additional comment letters. Modifications to the original Exposure Draft were made, and a second Exposure Draft was issued in July 1976. This time, the Board received 282 comment letters.

SFAS 13, "Accounting for Leases," was issued in November 1976. The FASB adopted a very detailed approach in response to demands from the

---

[2]Opinion 31 was the last one issued by the APB. Interestingly, it was actually issued in September 1973, several months after the APB was officially disbanded and while the FASB was already in operation. Perhaps to avoid confusion, the Opinion is dated June 1973.

profession for this type of specific guidance. As indicated in Chapter 3, accounting for leases continued to be an issue for the FASB. Altogether, the Board has issued seven Standards, six Interpretations, and ten Technical Bulletins on lease accounting. The issues were resurrected in 1984 as part of concerns over "standards overload," but the Board decided against adding the project to its agenda. This decision was popular with preparers because the apparent preliminary leaning of the Board was to capitalize all leases and thereby close off the loopholes that many corporations were using to leave liabilities off the balance sheet.

Pensions

A pension is a contract whereby an employer agrees to compensate its employees for work done in the present or past by making payments to them after they retire. In effect, it is argued, services are obtained from employees but paid for later. On the surface, it appears that the employer has a liability to its employees. However, an opportunity to employ off-balance-sheet financing could arise if the liability could be left out of the financial statements.

Indeed, that omission was the established practice for many years. APB Opinion 8, issued in 1966, made an attempt to have corporations place a liability on their balance sheets; however, application of the opinion did not result in the reporting of liabilities for pension obligations. The amounts omitted from the balance sheet grew very large, with the result that many statement preparers became even more strongly opposed to the idea of recognizing a liability than they were when Opinion 8 was developed. Others opposed recognizing the liability because they thought that the measurement of the amount payable to employees in the future was too uncertain and, as a result, too unreliable to merit recognition. This view was shared by many preparers, auditors, and users.

The FASB put employer accounting for pensions on its agenda in 1974 for two primary reasons. First, the Employees' Retirement Income Security Act of 1974 (ERISA) raised interest in pensions. Second, news articles identified the problem and criticized pension accounting and corporations with large amounts not reported as liabilities. Stopgap measures were issued in SFAS 35 on the financial statements for the actual pension plan (an entity legally separate from the employer) and in SFAS 36 on footnote disclosures of certain pension items. Both standards were issued in 1980.

In February 1981, the Board published a Discussion Memorandum on pensions and received 193 responses. In July 1981, the Board heard 37 presentations at public hearings. The FASB proposed recognition of a liability (net of investments committed to a pension investment fund) in a 1982 Preliminary Views document. This publication generated huge opposition from all quarters.

After more hearings and a very intensive effort to find compromises among themselves that would satisfy the vocal constituencies, four Board

Members agreed to issue SFAS 87 in December 1985. Incidentally, a delay in the vote beyond the end of the year would have brought into the project two new Board Members who would have to be familiarized with the issues; furthermore, trying to integrate their views might have overturned the majority.

SFAS 87 is very complicated because of the unfamiliar concepts that were used to develop it and the compromises that were reached. In brief, it requires pension expense to be calculated **as if** the employer has recognized not only a full pension liability, but also assets for the pension fund investments and a type of employee goodwill purchased by promising to pay them more in the future. However, the employer does not have to recognize more than a so-called minimum liability, which is far below the full amount. In addition, the Board invented techniques to arbitrarily smooth out income and defer the effects of changing to the new methods. The compromises were so rampant that the Board's explanation of the basis for its conclusions includes the highly unusual warning that, "...the most current and most relevant information [is excluded] from the employer's statement of financial position. That information is, however, included in the disclosures required [by the Statement]..." (par. 104). The Board also deferred implementation of SFAS 87 for several years with the result that its full effects cannot be evaluated in 1987.

The difficulty of completing the process will certainly keep pensions off the FASB's agenda for a number of years; however, the issues will inevitably come back again for another cut at some point in the future.

Unconsolidated Finance Subsidiaries

Another device that has been used to create off-balance-sheet financing is the **wholly owned subsidiary company**, which is often referred to as a "finance subsidiary." In legal form, the parent company owns an investment in the stock of the subsidiary. In economic substance, however, it owns the subsidiary's assets and is obligated by its liabilities.

If the financial statements were to be based on the form instead of the substance, the parent could cause the subsidiary to go into debt, and the new assets and liability would not be recognized on the parent's statement of financial position. For example, suppose that company has a balance sheet that looks like this (assume that the numbers are in millions):

Cash	$ 50	Debt		$300
Accounts receivable	200			
Other assets	350	Equity		300
Total	$600	Total		$600

Notice that the ratio of the debt to the equity is 1.00.

Now, suppose the management wants to borrow $200 million. If it does, its cash will go to $250 million, total assets will be $800 million, and the debt will be $500 million. As a consequence, its debt-equity ratio will go to an uncomfortably high 1.67.

As an alternative, the management sets up a new subsidiary corporation, and the parent corporation buys all of its stock for $1 million cash. The parent's balance sheet will appear as follows:

Cash	$ 49	Debt	$300
Accounts receivable	200		
Investment	1		
Other assets	350	Equity	300
Total	$600	Total	$600

Thus, there is no significant change in its apparent financial position.

At this point, the parent can have the subsidiary borrow the needed $200 million cash, which is transferred to the parent by "selling" the accounts receivable to the subsidiary. After this second event, the parent's balance sheet will look like this:

Cash	$249	Debt	$300
Accounts receivable	0		
Investment	1		
Other assets	350	Equity	300
Total	$600	Total	$600

Thus, the debt-equity ratio remains at 1.00, even though $200 million has been borrowed.

In contrast, suppose the accounting rules require the economic substance of the relationship between the parent and subsidiary to be the basis for the statements instead of the legal form. By this view, there would be no investment in stock on the parent's balance sheet, the sale of the receivables would not be treated as a real transaction, and the subsidiary's $200 million of debt would be considered to be the parent's liability. The **consolidated** balance sheet would look like this:

Cash	$250	Debt	$500
Accounts receivable	200		
Other assets	350	Equity	300
Total	$800	Total	$800

This picture is the same that would be presented if the subsidiary had never been created in the first place. Notice that the debt-equity ratio has climbed to 1.67 ($500 ÷ $300).

In most parent-subsidiary situations, this treatment is required because accountants have accepted the concept that the financial statements of the two companies should be *consolidated*. The reasonableness of this approach was so widely accepted that it was rarely debated. However, in the course of conducting a 1956 survey of accounting practices related to consolidations, the Research Department of the AICPA found that some companies were not consolidating the assets and debts of special finance subsidiaries like the one described above. Because the CAP's mandate was primarily to describe acceptable practices rather than to resolve controversies, it issued ARB 51 as a description of what many companies seemed to be doing about consolidations. With respect to the question of whether all subsidiaries should be consolidated, the Bulletin says without much explanation that it "may be preferable" to present separate statements for finance companies that have a parent company engaged in manufacturing.

This exception created a loophole in the eyes of many managers, with the result that a large number of finance subsidiaries were created in subsequent years. Furthermore, subsidiaries grew to the point that they dwarfed their parents. For example, the 1985 statement of financial position for General Motors shows debts of about $25 billion, compared to about $30 billion of stockholders' equity. Combining these figures gives a debt-equity ratio of 0.8. However, the primary financial statements for GM do not consolidate the assets and debts of its finance subsidiary, General Motors Acceptance Corporation (GMAC). By studying the footnotes, it can be determined that GMAC had debts of $70 billion and only $5 billion of equity. If these amounts had been consolidated, GM's debts would total around $95 billion, while equity would remain at $30 billion, and the debt-equity ratio would be about 3.2. The immense scale of the off-balance-sheet financing is quite apparent in this case.

In 1982, the FASB added a project to its agenda to consider a number of conceptual and practical issues related to the "accounting entity." Included among those issues was the question of whether the assets and liabilities of finance subsidiaries should be consolidated with those of the parent. In the fall of 1986, the Board issued an Exposure Draft of a Standard that would require the consolidation of all controlled subsidiaries without regard to the line of business. If it becomes effective, GM's financial statements will look quite different, although the real economic situation will not change.

INCOME TAXES

On the surface, accounting for income taxes seems to be a fairly straightforward problem. Once the tax for a given year is calculated on the tax return, it might appear that the amount should be recognized as an expense on the income statement. To the extent that the tax has not been paid or has been overpaid, a liability or a receivable would be recognized.

Deferred Taxes

It is not that simple, however, because of differences between the definitions of income under GAAP and under the tax code that put revenues (or expenses) in different time periods. That is, it is possible for a transaction to produce a revenue (or expense) on the current year's income statement under GAAP while no revenue (or expense) is recognized on the same year's tax return because the tax code would recognize it in some future period or periods. The result is that there is often no direct relationship between the amount of GAAP income for a year and the amount of tax actually paid.

This lack of correlation is of special concern to management because it would tend to produce volatility in reported after-tax income from year to year if the amount of tax computed on the tax return were to be the amount also reported as expense on the income statement. It is also of concern to users because a company can make an election for the tax return (such as accelerated depreciation) that merely *postpones* the payment of taxes rather than permanently reducing them. Thus, users are concerned that profits might be overstated and liabilities understated.

The earliest authoritative discussion of accounting for income taxes can be found in ARB 2 (issued in 1939), which dealt with accounting for refunded debt. The bulletin suggested that the cost of refunding debt should be amortized over the life of the debt. Because all of these refunding costs were deductible for tax purposes in the year of the refunding, it also indicated that there might be an effect for income taxes on the financial statements. It offered no suggestion, however, on how to account for this effect.

ARB 18, issued in 1942, also dealt with refunding of debt. This bulletin recognized the fact that the accounting for the refunding transaction might be different under GAAP than under the tax code. However, it offered a method of accounting for the effect on income taxes that would recognize the income tax expense in proportion to the reported income.

Another event that resulted in the discussion of accounting for income taxes was related to World War II. Specifically, the tax code allowed the cost of so-called emergency facilities to be written off over only five years on the tax return. ARB 27, issued in 1946, discussed how companies should account for the amortization and depreciation of these facilities. Additional material was included in ARB 42, issued in 1952, and then restated in ARB 43, which combined many previous bulletins, including ARB 23 dealing with various tax accounting issues. It discussed how to account for the tax effects of using a longer period of write-off for financial reporting than the five years allowed for tax purposes. The bulletin suggested a combination of the techniques now known as the "net of tax" and "liability" methods.

Accounting for income taxes was also discussed in ARB 44, "Declining-Balance Depreciation," which was issued in October 1954. Although the declining-balance method had been used in England for many years, its use in the United States had been limited. When the Internal Revenue Code of 1954 liberalized its acceptability for tax purposes, interest in its use grew significantly. ARB 44 identified the circumstances in which the use of declining-balance depreciation might be appropriate for financial reporting and suggested that accounting recognition might be given to the effects on income taxes when the declining-balance method was used for tax purposes and some other method of depreciation was used for the financial statements. It indicated, however, that such recognition was not necessary in ordinary situations.

In July 1958, a revised version of ARB 44 was issued. It addressed the tax issues related to accelerated depreciation more directly, and suggested that recognition be given to "deferred taxes" for amounts of tax on the current year's reported income that would be paid in the future. The members of the Committee on Accounting Procedure indicated that they had observed and studied cases involving the application of the original version of ARB 44 and had concluded that recognition of deferred taxes was needed to obtain an appropriate matching of costs and revenues and thereby avoid income distortion. Dissenters to the revised ARB 44 expressed their concern over the use of a bulletin on depreciation to create an accounting standard on deferred taxes.

After the release of the new ARB 44, questions were raised about the CAP's intent in using the phrase "deferred tax" for the account to be credited with the postponed income tax effects. In April 1959, the CAP issued an interpretation letter indicating that the account was meant to be either a "deferred credit" or a liability account but stating that it could not be reported as a credit to earned surplus (the previously acceptable term for "retained earnings") or any other stockholders' equity account. As a result, the AICPA was sued by Appalachian Power Company, which had been reporting the credit balances as adjustments to earned surplus. The case eventually went to the Supreme Court, with the AICPA prevailing.

In 1966, the APB released Accounting Research Study No. 9, "Interperiod Allocation of Corporate Income Taxes." This study led to the issuance of APB 11, "Accounting for Income Taxes," which was still the authoritative guideline on tax accounting in 1987. This opinion requires the use of the deferral method and reinforces the prohibition against increasing stockholders' equity for deferred taxes. Furthermore, it addresses other tax issues, including the treatment of the tax benefits arising from the deductibility of a current year's loss from prior and future years' taxable income. APB 11 also established the practice of **intraperiod** tax allocation, which disaggregates the total tax expense into portions associated with different categories of income identified on the income statement.

All in all, Opinion 11 proved highly acceptable for a number of years. However, the FASB began its own project on tax accounting in the early 1980s. One reason was the incompatibility of the deferred tax account with the Conceptual Framework's definitions of elements of financial statements in SFAC 3. A more persuasive reason was the growing criticism that Opinion 11's approach had become too complicated as a result of the increasing complexity of the tax law. Some felt that the ever-increasing size of the balance of deferred taxes on the statement of financial position invalidated the basic assumption that the account balance would decline as time passed.

The FASB's first step was a research report that identified many of the problems in reporting income taxes.[3] This publication was followed in 1983

---

[3] Dennis Beresford, et al., *Accounting for Income Taxes: A Review of Alternatives* (Stamford, Conn.: FASB, 1983).

by a Discussion Memorandum and public hearings. Very unexpectedly, the comment letters expressed satisfaction with the status quo. Generally, they reflected concern that the Board might actually make practice more complex or might bring back more volatility in reported income by simplifying the procedures. The preliminary decisions described in a 1986 Exposure Draft indicate that the FASB will continue many of the APB 11 procedures, with a few exceptions. The biggest change is the Board's proposal that the deferred taxes account be treated and recognized as a real liability instead of the previously used deferred credit that was neither a liability nor equity. This approach implies that the taxpayer's deferred tax liability should be adjusted up or down as soon as tax rates are changed; under the deferred approach, the effect of the rate change is spread over the future. A measurement implication of the liability approach is that the liability balance should be the present value of the expected future tax payments instead of the simple sum of the payments. The Board decided against implementing the discounting on the basis of simplicity; however, doing so does not reflect the advantages of postponing taxes, and thus presents an incomplete picture. This compromise seems to appeal to at least some members of the preparer community because it keeps their tax expense higher, and thereby reduces the likelihood that they will attract attention from the press and politicians for not paying their fair share of taxes. The final standard was slated for release in the third quarter of 1987.

The Investment Tax Credit

Another income tax–related accounting problem was the *investment tax credit,* which was a special onetime reduction in taxes that the taxpayer qualified for simply by buying particular types of assets (generally not real estate). The accounting issue was how to report the savings inherent in the tax credit. Three different positions were popular: (1) reduce the cost of the asset by the savings; (2) reduce tax expense in the year of the purchase; and (3) reduce tax expense over the life of the asset.

The APB attempted to deal with the investment tax credit in 1962 as an accounting issue instead of a political issue. Initially, the APB concluded in Opinion 2 that the first position (called "cost reduction") was most consistent with the traditional accounting model that attempts to spread benefits over the useful lives of assets. However, the APB had not reckoned with the political strength of corporate managers who wanted quick improvements in their reported profits. The investment tax credit was created to help stimulate business activity in the middle of a recession, when corporate profits were depressed. A number of corporate managers appealed to the SEC, which disagreed with the APB position. Only a few weeks after Opinion 2 was issued, the SEC stated in Accounting Series Release No. 96 that the second method (called "flowthrough") also was acceptable for financial statements filed with the Commission. Fifteen months later, the APB issued Opinion 4, which acknowledged that the flowthrough method was acceptable, as well as the cost reduction method and the third method listed above (called "deferral").

The investment tax credit lapsed, but it was restored by Congress in the early 1970s. At that time, the APB undertook another project to resolve the issue. Congress, however, included a provision in the Revenue Act of 1971 that a taxpayer could not be bound by anyone's decision as to how to present the savings from investment tax credits in the financial statements. This provision is generally considered to be the result of lobbying by strong corporate interests that were trying to protect their profit pictures. Consequently, the FASB could not meaningfully address the issue in its 1986 Exposure Draft. The Tax Reform Act of 1986 eliminated the investment tax credit and the issues were made moot. However, they will surface again if and when Congress decides that the credit should be restored.

CHANGING PRICES

Perhaps no other unresolved accounting issue has generated as much controversy and emotion as the one that asks whether financial statements should be based on the amounts originally spent and received or on measures that reflect the *current values* of the statement items. In fact, some evidence of disagreement appears in the literature as early as 1918.[4] If prices were stable, there would be no issue. Prices are anything but stable, however, and the controversy has attracted much attention.

Price-Level Adjustments

A middle-ground position is to keep the original cost amounts but to express them in terms of *constant dollars*. This process reflects only the effects of inflation, which is the change in the purchasing power of the dollar. The historical cost of an item is adjusted by a general price index that measures the change in purchasing power.

This price-level-adjusted approach tends to be popular with auditors because it allows them to continue using the same basic verification procedures that they use for traditional historical cost accounting systems. Price-level adjustments are not favored by preparers because the process usually increases the reported amounts of cost of goods sold and depreciation while leaving revenues unchanged. Thus, the amount of reported income is virtually always reduced. It also diminishes their apparent performance in operating the corporation by increasing assets and equity; this effect combines with the lower income level to produce a substantial reduction in the return on assets.

---

[4]Livingston Middleditch, "Should Accounts Reflect the Changing Value of the Dollar?" *Journal of Accountancy,* February 1918, pp. 114–20.

A complete description of price-level adjustments was articulated by Henry Sweeney in the 1930s.[5] The widespread interest in the problem is reflected in the fact that the Rockefeller Foundation funded a study during the 1940s by a group of accountants, economists, labor leaders, and bankers on business income, including alternative methods for reflecting the effects of inflation.

The APB considered the possibility of requiring price-level-adjusted financial statements but could not get the two-thirds majority needed to make them mandatory. The nonauthoritative APB Statement 3 was issued in 1969 and recommended that historical cost financial statements be supplemented by general price-level-adjusted information. Its recommendations were almost totally ignored.

The FASB added accounting for changing prices to its agenda and issued an Exposure Draft in 1974 that would have required price-level-adjusted information in the footnotes to the financial statements. But, the SEC intervened in 1976 by issuing Accounting Series Release No. 190, which required the largest registrants to provide a different type of disclosure based on current values.

The Board deferred issuing a statement on price-level-adjusted (or "constant dollar") accounting until it had progressed further on its Conceptual Framework project (discussed in the next chapter) and until additional studies and hearings could be held on the issues. In 1979, the Board issued SFAS 33, "Financial Reporting and Changing Prices," which put the technique of price-level adjustments into use as supplemental information (the standard also included current value requirements). However, the constant dollar requirements were dropped from the standard when it became apparent that the approach lacked support from any constituent group. This was accomplished late in 1984 through SFAS 82.

Current Value

In contrast to price-level adjustments, the **current value** approach would report the changed price of an item whether the change was related to inflation or to shifts in specific prices. The intent of this approach is to reflect the results of changes in the supply and demand for particular items, and it is supported on the basis that it provides more complete information. For example, if an item cost $1 when purchased and inflation over the next year is 10 percent, price-level adjustments would report the item at $1.10. However, because of a low supply of the item (or a high demand for it), the current value of the item might be $1.15. Thus, neither the original cost nor the price-level-adjusted amount would provide complete information about the item.

Using current value creates a need to recognize so-called holding gains and losses, which arise from owning assets when prices increase or decrease

---

[5]Henry W. Sweeney, *Stabilized Accounting* (New York: Harper & Row, 1936).

(the opposite happens when liabilities are owed). This approach tends to be unpopular with auditors because it forces verification of amounts not determined through transactions involving the client company and would create uncertainty and risk for them.

Preparers tend to argue against the use of current values because it causes them to incur the costs of implementing a new accounting system. It also causes them to lose control over some of the information that flows to users. Furthermore, it tends to create fluctuations in reported income as values change. Perhaps most significantly, it causes them to report lower income from operations because the cost of goods sold and depreciation expense tend to be higher.

Despite the many arguments raised in favor of the current value approach, it was not accepted as part of common practice until SFAS 33 was issued in 1979. This standard created a partial application of the approach by requiring the reporting of supplemental current value information by approximately 1,500 large public corporations that met specified size criteria. As described in Chapter 5, the issue of whether current values should be used more extensively eventually became the focus for the recognition and measurement phase of the Conceptual Framework project.

Because of the cautious posture adopted by the Board in Statement of Financial Accounting Concepts No. 5, it appeared unlikely that much would be done to increase the use of current values. However, perhaps because of some membership changes, the Board made the following announcement in the October 8, 1985, issue of *Status Report:*

> The Board has concluded that the information about the effects of inflation and changes in specific prices is important in assessing the amounts, timing, and uncertainty of prospective cash flows. The Board also agrees that the present requirements for the disclosure of the effects of changing prices has not met that need. As a result, the Board has determined it should continue to strive to improve the disclosures and has tentatively approved a continuing agenda project having the objective of developing more effective and useful disclosures of the impact of changing prices on enterprise performance, resources, obligations, and financial capital. The FASB staff is working to develop the scope and content of that project.
>
> The Board has concluded that the present disclosure requirement contained in Statement 33, "Financial Reporting and Changing Prices," as amended, should be retained during the continuing agenda project period.

Despite this resolve in 1985, the coalition of Board Members supporting current value experimentation fell apart late in 1986 in frustration over finding a direction for future development. Shortly thereafter, SFAS 89 was issued, and changed the remaining requirements of SFAS 33 to voluntary guidelines to be used by those preparers who wanted to provide the information. Given the approach's lack of popularity with preparers, undoubtedly few if any of them will publish the numbers.

As this history shows, of course, this action by the FASB will not make the issue disappear. It will be there the next time the economy experiences significant inflation or a significant change in supply and demand functions. At that time, yet another outcry will be made for accountants to do something with the financial statements to reflect changing prices. The abandonment of SFAS 33 will make responding to this pressure more difficult, in the words of Board Member David Mosso's dissent to SFAS 89:

> Although Statement 33 had obvious shortcomings, it was a base on which to build. It represented years of due process—research, debate, deliberations, decisions—and application experience. As last amended, it had made significant progress in eliminating alternative concepts and methodologies. Its recision means that much of that due process and application experience will have to be repeated in response to a future inflation crisis. That will entail great cost in terms of time, money, and creative talent, and, because due process does not permit quick reaction to crises, it risks loss of credibility for the Board and loss of initiative in private sector standard setting.

Perhaps those who fail to learn from history are doomed to repeat it.

SUMMARY

The FASB has faced numerous controversies during its lifetime. Some originated then, but many were merely new forms of controversies that existed earlier. By being familiar with the history of some of these issues, the readers will find it easier to cope with new issues that emerge and they will be more capable of evaluating the adequacy of newly proposed solutions.

SELECTED READINGS

BARTLEY, JON W., and LEWIS S. DAVIDSON. "The Entity Concept and Accounting for Interest Costs." *Accounting and Business Research,* Summer 1982, pp. 175–87.

BURNS, GARY W., and D. SCOTT PETERSON. "Accounting for Computer Software." *Journal of Accountancy,* April 1982, pp. 50–58.

GRUBE, CORWIN, and HUGO NURNBERG. "Alternative Methods of Accounting for Business Combinations." *The Accounting Review,* October 1970, pp. 783–89.

HENDRICKSEN, ELDON S. *Accounting Theory.* 4th ed. Homewood, Ill.: Richard D. Irwin, 1982.

MILLER, PAUL B. W. "The New Pension Accounting (Part 1)." *The Journal of Accountancy,* January 1987, pp. 98–108.

NAIR, R. D., and J. J. WEYGANDT. "Let's Fix Deferred Taxes." *Journal of Accountancy,* November 1981, pp. 87–102.

RAYBURN, FRANK R. "Discounting of Deferred Income Taxes: An Argument for Reconsideration." *Accounting Horizons,* March 1987, pp. 43–50.

SCHIPPER, KATHERINE, and ROMAN WEIL. "Alternative Accounting Treatments for Pensions." *The Accounting Review,* October 1982, pp. 806–24.

SUNDER, SHYAM. "Properties of Accounting Numbers under Full Costing and Successful Efforts Costing in the Petroleum Industry." *The Accounting Review,* January 1976, pp. 1–18.

VANCIL, RICHARD F. "Inflation Accounting—The Great Controversy." *Harvard Business Review,* March–April 1976, pp. 58–67.

PUBLICATION REFERENCES

AMERICAN INSTITUTE OF CPAs

Committee on Accounting Procedure—Accounting Research Bulletins:

No. 2   Unamortized Discount and Redemption Premium on Bonds Refunded, September 1939

No. 18   Unamortized Discount and Redemption Premium on Bonds Refunded (Supplement), December 1942

No. 23   Accounting for Income Taxes, December 1944

No. 27   Emergency Facilities, November 1946

No. 38   Disclosure of Long-Term Leases in Financial Statements of Lessees, October 1949

No. 42   Emergency Facilities: Depreciation, Amortization, and Income Taxes, November 1952

No. 43   Restatement and Revision of Accounting Research Bulletins, June 1953

No. 44   Declining-Balance Depreciation, October 1954

No. 44   (Revised) Declining-Balance Depreciation, July 1958

No. 51   Consolidated Financial Statements, August 1959

Accounting Principles Board—Opinions:

No. 2   Accounting for the "Investment Credit," December 1962

No. 4   (Amending No. 2) Accounting for the "Investment Credit," March 1964

No. 5   Reporting of Leases in Financial Statements of Lessee, September 1964

No. 7   Accounting for Leases in Financial Statements of Lessors, May 1966

No. 8   Accounting for the Cost of Pension Plans, November 1966

No. 11   Accounting for Income Taxes, December 1967

No. 27   Accounting for Lease Transactions by Manufacturer or Dealer Lessors, November 1972

No. 31   Disclosure of Lease Commitments by Lessees, June 1973

Accounting Principles Board—Statement:

No. 3   Financial Statements Restated for General Price-Level Changes, June 1969

Accounting Research Studies:

No. 4   John H. Myers, "Reporting of Leases in Financial Statements," 1962

No. 9   Homer A. Black, "Interperiod Allocation of Corporate Income Taxes," 1966

No. 14   Oscar S. Gellein and Maurice S. Newman, "Accounting for Research and Development Expenditures," 1973

FINANCIAL ACCOUNTING STANDARDS BOARD

Statements of Financial Accounting Standards

No. 2   Accounting for Research and Development Costs, October 1974

No. 13   Accounting for Leases, November 1976

No. 19   Financial Accounting and Reporting by Oil and Gas Producing Companies, December 1977

No. 25   Suspension of Certain Accounting Requirements for Oil and Gas Producing Companies (an amendment of FASB Statement No. 19), February 1979

No. 33   Financial Reporting and Changing Prices, September 1979

No. 34   Capitalization of Interest Cost, October 1979

No. 35   Accounting and Reporting by Defined Benefit Pension Plans

No. 36   Disclosure of Pension Information (an amendment of APB Opinion No. 8), May 1980

No. 69   Disclosures about Oil and Gas Producing Activities (an amendment of FASB Statements 19, 25, 33, and 39), November 1982

No. 82   Financial Reporting and Changing Prices: Elimination of Certain Disclosures (an amendment of FASB Statement No. 33), November 1984

No. 86   Accounting for the Costs of Computer Software to Be Sold, Leased, or Otherwise Marketed, August 1985

No. 87   Employers' Accounting for Pensions, December 1985

No. 89   Financial Reporting and Changing Prices, December 1986

Exposure Drafts of Statements of Financial Accounting Standards

Financial Reporting in Units of General Purchasing Power, December 1974

Accounting for Income Taxes, September 1986
Consolidation of All Majority-Owned Subsidiaries, December 1986

Statement of Financial Accounting Concepts

No. 3   Elements of Financial Statements of Business Enterprises, December 1980

No. 5   Recognition and Measurement in Financial Statements of Business Enterprises, December 1984

Interpretation

No. 6   Applicability of FASB Statement No. 2 to Computer Software (an interpretation of FASB Statement No. 2), February 1975

Discussion Documents

Discussion Memorandum—An Analysis of Issues Related to Accounting for Research and Development Costs, 1973

Discussion Memorandum—An Analysis of Issues Related to Accounting for Leases, 1974

Discussion Memorandum—An Analysis of Issues Related to Accounting for Pensions and Other Post-Employment Benefits, 1981

Preliminary Views on Major Issues Related to Employers' Accounting for Pensions and Other Postemployment Benefits, 1982

Discussion Memorandum—An Analysis of Issues Related to Accounting for Income Taxes, 1983

SECURITIES AND EXCHANGE COMMISSION

Accounting Series Releases

No. 96   Accounting for the "Investment Tax Credit," 1963

No. 132   Reporting Leases in Financial Statements of Lessees, 1973

No. 141   Interpretations and Minor Amendments Applicable to Certain Revisions of Regulation S-X, 1973

No. 147   Notice of Adoption of Amendments to Regulation S-X Requiring Improved Disclosure of Leases, 1973

No. 190   Notice of Adoption of Amendments to Regulation S-X Requiring Disclosure of Certain Replacement Cost Data, 1976

No. 253   Adoption of Requirements for Financial Accounting and Reporting Practices for Oil and Gas Producing Activities, 1978

No. 257   Requirements for Financial Accounting and Reporting Practices for Oil and Gas Producing Activities, 1978

No. 259   Oil and Gas Producers—Full Cost Accounting Practices, 1978

REVIEW QUESTIONS

1. What is the fundamental issue regarding capitalization versus expensing?

2. Preferences for capitalization or expensing differ among those interested in financial statements. Describe the general preferences of preparers, users, and auditors.

3. What two factors contribute to the capitalization versus expensing controversy in accounting for the costs of research and development?

4. Identify the event that led the APB to begin studying accounting for research and development costs.

5. Describe the treatment of research and development costs as specified in SFAS 2.

6. State the primary reason for capitalizing interest costs.

7. Why did utility companies begin capitalizing interest cost before other corporations?

8. SFAS 34 requires the capitalization of interest costs associated with what kinds of activities?

9. What caused software companies to prefer capitalization of development costs?

10. Discuss the similarities and differences between software development costs and research and development costs and between the accounting treatments prescribed for them.

11. Summarize the major differences between the successful efforts and full-cost accounting methods used by oil and gas companies.

12. In the 1970s, the SEC took a more active role in establishing accounting policy for oil and gas companies. What events brought on the SEC's involvement, and what was the nature of its action?

13. The SEC's proposal for accounting for the exploration activities of oil and gas companies was reserve recognition accounting (RRA). In some respects, it is a rather novel approach to the capitalization versus expensing problem. Describe RRA accounting, and characterize the accounting profession's general reaction to it.

14. What is the possible benefit for a company in arranging off-balance-sheet financing?

15. Explain how leasing can be used by a lessee to obtain the benefits of an off-balance-sheet financing arrangement.

16. Under ARB 38, what disclosures concerning leased assets were to be made?

17. What were the two primary reasons that caused the FASB to place pensions on its agenda in 1974?

18. Provide arguments for and against recognizing a pension liability on the balance sheet.

19. What is one major advantage of not consolidating a subsidiary?

20. What type of subsidiary of a manufacturing company is often not consolidated?

21. What causes the income taxes of a company for a given year to be different on the financial statements and on the tax return?

22. Define deferred taxes.

23. Provide three reasons why the FASB undertook an income taxes project.

24. What was the investment tax credit, and what accounting issues did it create?

25. What precluded the FASB from limiting acceptable methods of accounting for investment tax credits?

26. Name and describe the two alternatives to historical cost accounting that account for changing prices.

27. In using the current value approach, holding gains arise. What are holding gains, and why do auditors face difficulty in auditing them?

28. What was the purpose of SFAS 82?

EXERCISES

1. The following chart presents the agenda of the FASB as of July 1987. The chart indicates each project and its status. Determine the current status of the projects and update the chart. Also include new projects added to the agenda.

Project	Status as of July 1987	Status as of _____
1. Income taxes	Further deliberations	
2. Stock compensation	Early deliberations	
3. Cash flow reporting	Further deliberations	
4. Consolidation of majority owned subsidiaries	Further deliberations	
5. Financial instruments	Early deliberations	
6. Postemployment benefits other than pensions	Early deliberations	

2. This chapter included a discussion of four areas of accounting controversies: capitalization versus expensing, off-balance-sheet financing, income taxes, and changing prices. Review your additions to the agenda in Exercise 1, and identify whether any of the new projects are related to these controversies.

3. A history of four accounting controversies was included in this chapter to demonstrate the role of people and politics in the process for setting standards. Select (or your instructor might assign) one of the following accounting issues, and prepare a brief history of the controversy. The issues are: foreign currency accounting, components of income (current operating versus all inclusive approaches), and extinguishments of debt.

4. Obtain one or more *Intermediate Accounting* or *Accounting Theory* textbooks and find their discussions of several of the issues described in this chapter. Analyze the presentations to determine whether the issues and their resolutions are described in terms of political or theoretical factors, or both. Do the descriptions correspond to those presented in this book? Try to explain any differences that you uncover. Can you think of any reasons that might cause textbook authors to leave out politics in their discussions of these and other issues?

5

The Conceptual
Framework Project

This chapter provides a closer examination of the Conceptual Framework, which is widely considered the single most important project in the FASB's history. Its importance is indicated by several facts. First, it was placed on the initial agenda created by the Board in 1973, with high expectations for its accomplishments. Second, it led to the publication of six Statements of Financial Accounting Concepts. Third, it involved a long and complex set of due process procedures, including five Discussion Memoranda, a Tentative Conclusions document, seven Exposure Drafts, a series of eight Research Studies, and six public hearings. Fourth, it generated substantial controversy among Board Members, Staff Members, and the FASB constituencies. Finally, and most significantly, the project was given the goal of laying the foundation for future directions in setting standards. A critical evaluation of the project is included in this book because many observers have argued that the Framework has not met the expectations that were established at its inception. Some have asserted that it is a failure, and some have called it a disappointment. Still others consider it a success.

In dealing with the Conceptual Framework, this chapter presents three sections:

- The reasons for having a conceptual framework and approaches to developing one.
- The FASB's experience.
- A summary and evaluation of the contents of the concepts statements.

THE REASONS FOR HAVING A CONCEPTUAL FRAMEWORK AND APPROACHES TO DEVELOPING ONE

In any field of study or activity, including financial accounting, there are a number of reasons for developing a "conceptual framework," which is a collection of broad rules, guidelines, accepted truths, and other basic ideas. The following three reasons for creating such a framework are discussed in this section:

- Description of existing practice.
- Prescription of future practices.
- Definition of commonly used terms.

[handwritten: Consistency of standards / Validity of deduction]

Description of Existing Practice

[handwritten: confused — mixing education with description]

One main goal of developing a conceptual framework that describes existing practice is to make it easier to **educate** nonaccountants about what it is that accountants do. This education may occur for the purpose of training new accountants or simply for helping nonaccountants understand how to use accounting information. Another goal of the description may be to help standard setters solve new problems by stating general rules that are followed for existing similar transactions, events, or conditions. By relating the new problems to previously encountered ones and then reasoning by analogy, it may be possible to come up with solutions that are acceptable because they appear to be consistent with those that are already in use. *[handwritten: confused]*

The basic approach to developing a **descriptive** framework starts by examining what is being done in practice and then moves to higher level abstractions. As symbolized in Exhibit 5–1, the approach can be called **bottom-up**; a more technical term that is used to describe it is **inductive**.

Advantages and disadvantages. One advantage of the descriptive approach is its tendency to produce practical concepts that take into consideration the real-world problems leading to existing practices. For example, a

[handwritten: technical?]

[handwritten: mixing consistency with practice — fact: current practice is inconsistent!]

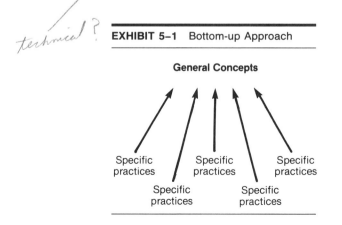

EXHIBIT 5–1 Bottom-up Approach

General Concepts

Specific practices
Specific practices
Specific practices
Specific practices
Specific practices

reliable measure!
Confused - mixing with evaluation

descriptive framework might include the concept that a corporation should not recognize its human resources as an asset because there are no reliable measures of their value; thus, other intangible assets can be recognized because they can be measured.

As briefly discussed in Chapter 1, many accountants want existing practices to be kept intact because, among other things, if there are no changes, they will not have to learn any new techniques and they will not lose control over the information reported to their corporations' stockholders. When this attitude is combined with the fact that a descriptive conceptual framework captures the essence of the status quo, the descriptive approach is widely preferred because it protects practice against changes. For example, if a descriptive concept is established that assets are recognized at cost, it will be fairly difficult to argue persuasively that a new standard should require a new type of asset to be reported at market value. Whether this protective effect is really an advantage depends, of course, on one's belief about the status quo. To those who want it maintained, the approach is advantageous; to those who favor change, the approach is not advantageous. As described later in the chapter, the conflict over the suitability of the status quo had a very significant effect on the FASB's efforts to establish its Conceptual Framework.

Regardless of one's position on the desirability of change, a major disadvantage of the descriptive approach is that it depends on observations of what is actually happening. Two problems arise from this dependence. First, an assumption must be made that the activity being observed is the right thing to do. That is, the observer has to conclude that a technique used in practice is the best that can ever be used. In fact, all that can be legitimately concluded is that the technique is merely **used**; it is not valid to conclude that it is the **most useful** technique or even that it is **useful at all**. Second, the development of a descriptive framework depends on obtaining agreement among a number of observers not only about **what** is actually happening but also (and more important) about **why** it is happening. In a sense, developing a descriptive framework is like giving several people an answer and then telling them to guess what the question is. It does not take much experience to know that there will be significant differences of opinion among them. For example, a number of people may agree that accountants initially recognize an asset at the amount paid for it. However, that agreement does not necessarily extend to the **reason** for using that amount. Some might argue that the accountants are interested in the original *cost* as a measure of the amount invested in the asset; on the other hand, others might assert that the amount paid is merely a very reliable estimate of the asset's *fair market value* on the purchase date. It is very difficult to determine why they do what they do, but it is precisely the reason why it is done that is important for the conceptual framework.

For another example, it can be observed from practice that inventories are commonly presented in the statement of financial position at cost, except for agricultural products, which are presented at market value. Without making an assumption, it is not possible to determine whether the general rule is to use cost or market. If cost is the desired goal, then the treatment of agricultural products is the exception and cost should be used for new types of inventories. Alternatively, if market is the desired goal, but cost is substituted when market is not reliably measured, then the treatment of agricultural products is not an exception.

Descriptive accounting frameworks. Because of these problems, widely accepted and useful descriptive frameworks for financial accounting have proven difficult to develop. Three examples of efforts to compile such frameworks are:

- *An Introduction to Corporate Accounting Standards,* written by William A. Paton and A. C. Littleton and published in 1940 by the American Accounting Association.
- *Accounting Research Study No. 7: An Inventory of Generally Accepted Accounting Principles,* written by Paul Grady and published by the AICPA in 1965.
- *Accounting Principles Board Statement No. 4: Basic Concepts and Accounting Principles Underlying Financial Statements of Business Enterprises,* developed by the APB and published by the AICPA in 1970.

Because these documents were descriptive, the concepts they contain often do not help a standards-setting body accomplish its mission; instead, a different type of framework is needed.

Prescription of Future Practices

In contrast to description, an important reason for developing an accounting conceptual framework is to provide guidance to help resolve old and new unsettled questions. There are at least two ways in which such a **prescriptive** framework can be helpful.

First, the guidance in its concepts can be for the benefit of a **formal standards-setting body** such as the APB or the FASB. Toward this end, the Accounting Principles Board made several attempts to develop a set of concepts, but it did not succeed in obtaining the guidance it sought.[1] Second, that guidance can help **individual practicing accountants** resolve reporting problems that are not covered by authoritative pronouncements.

A prescriptive framework is developed by starting with a few general concepts and working down through their implications to statements of what ought to be done in practice. As shown by the direction of the arrows in Exhibit 5–2, this approach is often called **top-down**; more technical terms that are used to describe this approach are **deductive** and **normative**.

---

[1]For a description of these efforts and their effect on the FASB's project, see Paul A. Pacter, "The Conceptual Framework: Make No Mystique about It," *Journal of Accountancy,* July 1983, pp. 76–88.

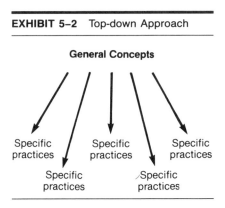

EXHIBIT 5–2 Top-down Approach

General Concepts

Specific practices

Specific practices

Specific practices

Specific practices

Specific practices

A prescriptive approach assumes a "clean slate," in the sense that it attempts to define the objectives of and limits on an activity without being constrained to include what is already being done or to exclude what is not being done.

Advantages and disadvantages. Because a prescriptive framework is not based on the assumption that what is being done is right, it offers the advantage of uncovering areas in existing practice that can be improved. To many accountants, of course, this feature is not an advantage because they want to keep the status quo in place without major changes.

A second advantage of a prescriptive framework is that it tends to produce simpler concepts that do not attempt to include all the intricacies of existing practice. For example, a prescriptive concept might state that all inventories should be carried at the most reliably estimated measure of their market value (one of which might be its cost). If both the cost and market of a new type of inventory are available (and they are different), there is no confusion as to how it should be accounted for. This concept is far different from a descriptive rule that says inventories are *usually* reported at their cost but are *sometimes* reported at their market value.

Another advantage of the top-down approach is that the developer of the framework does not have to carry any preexisting theories into it. At any point, the relevant question to be answered is whether the suggested lower level practice is consistent with the higher level concepts, and the developer does not need to be concerned about what *is* being done in practice. This approach tends to bring more rigor to standards setting because the usefulness of any procedure (new *or* old) should be proven before it is accepted as useful. In short, there is no presumption of usefulness simply because a practice is used.

Yet another advantage of a prescriptive framework is that its lack of ties to the status quo means that prescriptive rules can be more easily applied to new situations. In other words, reasoning by analogy is used less extensively when a prescriptive framework is applied than when a descriptive framework is applied. Additionally, a prescriptive framework is not made obsolete as soon as a new situation arises, whereas a descriptive framework must be modified to include the new practices that stem from that situation.

Of course, there are disadvantages to prescriptive frameworks. For one, they are difficult to compile because it is necessary to construct a consensus on the question of what accounting **ought** to accomplish. In effect, the top-down approach forces the resolution of all problems at the same time instead of providing the luxury of dealing with them one at a time. For example, if a proposed concept suggested that all assets should be measured in terms of their market values, it would be necessary to deal with this concept's implications for receivables, investments, inventory, operating assets, and intangibles and in all industries. In contrast, if each area and industry were tackled more or less independently, the affected constituent groups would be smaller and more easily satisfied.

A second disadvantage of prescriptive frameworks is that their concepts may be perceived as being so abstract as to be inapplicable. A typical reaction of practitioners to such frameworks is that they come from an "ivory tower" that has an artificial view of the "real world."

Prescriptive accounting frameworks. Several prescriptive frameworks for financial accounting have been attempted; among them are:

- *Accounting Research Study No. 1: The Basic Postulates of Accounting,* written by Maurice Moonitz and published by the AICPA in 1961, and *Accounting Research Study No. 3: A Tentative Set of Broad Accounting Principles,* written by Robert T. Sprouse and Moonitz and published by the AICPA in 1962. (Both of these studies were discussed in Chapter 2.)
- *A Statement of Basic Accounting Theory,* written by a committee of the American Accounting Association and published by the AAA in 1966.
- *Objectives of Financial Statements,* written by the Trueblood Study Group and published by the AICPA in 1973.

When this list is combined with the list of descriptive frameworks provided earlier on page 111, it can be seen that the APB and the AICPA had a particularly difficult time determining which approach was preferable for meeting their needs. Without a strong commitment to one of these approaches, there was only a low likelihood that success would be achieved.

Definition of Commonly Used Terms

A conceptual framework that defines commonly used terms is helpful to a standards-setting system (like the FASB) that involves deliberations and due process procedures. There are two main advantages. First, the processes can become more efficient because all the participants have the same definitions for the words that they use in communicating with each other. Second, a fixed set of definitions is more likely to help the new standards be consistent.

The main disadvantage of a framework that merely defines terms is that it will not eliminate debates. For example, Statement of Financial Accounting Concepts No. 3 defines assets as

> probable future economic benefits obtained or controlled by a particular entity as a result of past transactions or events. (par. 19)

Although the definition appears to be reasonable and straightforward, a more careful analysis shows that its meaning depends in turn on the meanings of such words as *probable, future, economic, benefits, obtained, controlled, entity, result, past, transaction,* and *events.* Because the definitions of these other terms can be debated, they will be used by participants in the due process to make their points or to attack the opponents' arguments. Although the definitions will not end the debates, they will at least focus them on a smaller set of issues. Eventually, as these issues are settled over and over again, common meanings will become established and the process will become more efficient.

In order to have wide acceptance, the definitions in this type of framework have to be developed through a political process that involves a number of parties. Thus, neither a strict prescriptive nor a pure descriptive approach is likely to be effective. Instead, some combination will have to be applied.

No accounting conceptual framework has been developed simply for the purpose of defining the terms to be used in setting standards. Of course, a number of publications provide definitions of accounting words, but they are more like dictionaries than theoretical structures.[2] Furthermore, they have not been put together for the purpose of guiding a standards-setting body.

Summary

In general, there are three purposes for developing a conceptual framework: to **describe** existing practices, to **prescribe** future practices, and to **define** commonly used terms. The preceding discussion of these purposes and of the approaches to developing frameworks that serve them has shown that they are very much in conflict. For example, a description of **existing practice** often does not provide a good prescription for dealing with **new transactions**. This point is especially important because it is very difficult (if not impossible) to obtain a consensus on the contents of a framework if those who are developing it do not agree on which purpose is to be served. The following section describes what happened to the FASB's project and shows how this lack of agreement as to its purpose played a significant role in the difficulties that

---

[2]For example, W. W. Cooper and Yuji Ijiri, eds., *Kohler's Dictionary for Accountants,* 6th ed. (Englewood Cliffs, N.J.: Prentice-Hall, 1983).

were encountered and in shaping the compromise nature of the statements that were produced.

THE FASB'S EXPERIENCE

Section III(H)(2) of the FASB's Rules of Procedure describes the goals of the Board's Conceptual Framework project by listing the following purposes for Statements of Financial Accounting Concepts:

- establish objectives and concepts that the Standards Board will use in developing standards of financial accounting and reporting;
- provide guidance in resolving problems of financial accounting and reporting that are not addressed in authoritative pronouncements; and
- enhance the assessment by users of the content and limitations of information provided by financial accounting and reporting and thereby further the ability to use that information effectively.

The first two purposes clearly establish that the FASB's Conceptual Framework was intended to be **prescriptive**, while the third purpose points out the **educational** goal. Nothing is said in this description about using a framework for **defining terms**.

In reflection of the priority on prescription, the Board's project was designed to be a top-down framework. It started with the identification of the highest level concept of what accounting is to accomplish, and it was then to move down through lower levels.

Not surprisingly, the project proved very controversial. A large part of the controversy stemmed from the fact that many constituents prefer the status quo and do not want a prescriptive framework because it implies change. More controversy arose because of the need for the shapers of a prescriptive framework to resolve a lot of issues at the same time. Specifically, the Board found it difficult to resolve *any* issues because at least some constituents criticized the Board on every stand it took. Virtually every issue had a high priority for some influential group, and a vigorous defense of the status quo was mounted everywhere the Board turned. With opposition from so many different directions, the Board did not have much room for the compromising that is so essential to the development of a consensus on the issues.

As a result of this opposition, the Board had to move back and forth between the prescriptive and descriptive approaches, as demonstrated in Statement of Financial Accounting Concepts No. 1 (SFAC 1). First, paragraph 34 identifies the primary objective of financial accounting and reporting[3] as

---

[3]The FASB decided to use the phrase "financial accounting and reporting" instead of only "financial accounting" because the Board Members wanted to acknowledge that much of the information presented *with* the financial statements is as important as the information that is presented *in* them. For fear that the term *accounting* might be too narrowly interpreted, they chose to add the additional words *and reporting* to assure that the wider scope of the Board's authority would be clearly stated.

providing useful information to creditors, investors, and others for rational decision making. Paragraph 37 explains that such decision making involves the users' assessments of the amount, timing, and uncertainty of cash flows from the enterprise to them. Paragraph 39 explains that these assessments depend on assessments of the cash flows of the enterprise itself. This series of conclusions might suggest (on a **prescriptive** basis) that the most useful information to report would be based directly on the entity's cash flows. But a **descriptive** discussion in paragraphs 44–48 very carefully defends traditional accrual accounting on the basis that it provides better data for assessing the enterprise's cash flows than does simple cash flow information. By including these comments, the Board alleviated fears that the prescriptive approach was going to produce a revolution in accounting practice.

Further into the project, the compromise between descriptive and prescriptive had advanced to the stage that the thrust of the project had become essentially descriptive. For example, paragraph 70 of SFAC 5 says:

> Rather than attempt to characterize present practice as being based on a single attribute with numerous exceptions for diverse reasons, this concepts statement characterizes present practice as based on different attributes.

If the project had been truly prescriptive, there would have been no need for the Board to attempt to characterize present practice in any way. The quote shows that the purpose of the framework had essentially become description rather than prescription of guidance for setting standards.

As a result of this compromising on the basic nature of the Conceptual Framework project, its output is neither very prescriptive nor descriptive but a combination that may be unsatisfactory for either purpose. Nonetheless, its output is useful because it defines a number of important terms that the Board can use in its internal and external communications. The terms also force constituents to be more rigorous in putting together their responses to discussion documents and Exposure Drafts. This accomplishment is somewhat ironic in light of the fact the Board never explicitly identified it as a goal for the project.

The Basic Steps in the FASB's Conceptual Framework Project

As mentioned earlier, the Conceptual Framework project was on the early agenda of the FASB. The project's first Discussion Memorandum, published in 1974, concerned the Trueblood Study Group's Report on the Objectives of Financial Statements. A second Discussion Memorandum, on measurement and the elements (or components) of financial statements, was published in 1976. Hearings on these documents took place in 1974 and 1977. The first Exposure Draft for the project was distributed in 1977, and SFAC 1 was issued in 1978. As described later in this chapter, this statement put users' needs at the head of the list of those to be served by financial accounting. Although this idea does not seem particularly revolutionary in retrospect, it can be interpreted as an official recognition of the shift to user interests and away from the orientation toward auditors' needs that had dominated standards setting since 1938.

Over the next two years, the project progressed through two more Exposure Drafts, and SFAC 2 and SFAC 3 were issued in 1980. SFAC 2 describes the qualities of information that is useful to the decision makers specified in SFAC 1 as important. These "qualitative characteristics" include relevance, reliability, and comparability, as well as several subcharacteristics that lead to the presence of these three. SFAC 3 identifies the elements of financial statements, which are the objects that the information should be about. They include such familiar items as assets, liabilities, owners' equity, revenues, and expenses. In 1980, the Board also issued SFAC 4, which adapted the objectives of SFAC 1 to nonbusiness entities, including universities, hospitals, charities, museums, and religious organizations, but not governmental organizations.

After this progress, the FASB ran into some difficulties in making the Conceptual Framework more specific. In particular, it ran up against opposition after issuing an Exposure Draft of a concepts statement concerned with the structure of the financial statements.[4] The primary trigger for the opposition was the Board's decision to focus on a broadly defined concept of income called **comprehensive income** instead of the more familiar concept of **earnings**. As a consequence of this focus, many constituents concluded that the FASB was proposing a revolutionary shift toward using many more current value measurements. This controversy put even more pressure on the "recognition and measurement" phase of the project.

Recognition and measurement. The goal of the recognition and measurement phase was to establish the very important concepts of *what* to put in the financial statements, *when* to put them there, and *what* amounts to associate with them. To many constituents, Board Members, and others, these issues seemed to be merely another way of raising the age-old (and deeply emotional) question of whether historical cost or current value should be the primary basis for measurement.

The phase started out with hopes for progress, although many constituents and at least some Board Members had become wary of the direction in which it seemed to be heading. One consideration that seemed to concern many was the appointment of Dr. Robert R. Sterling to the staff for a two-year term as "Senior Fellow." Dr. Sterling was a highly regarded academician with a reputation as a strong advocate of current values, particularly those representing the selling prices of assets.

---

[4] "Reporting Income, Cash Flows, and Financial Position of Business Enterprises," Proposed Statement of Financial Accounting Concepts, FASB, November 16, 1981.

The strategy adopted by the Staff and Board was to submit a series of case studies to the Board Members for discussion in meetings. Each case was designed to solicit an expression by each Board Member of what he thought on the specific issues, with the intermediate goal of identifying his individual internal framework concerning recognition and measurement. Then, the staff would try to identify those areas in which there was a consensus and move forward to an Exposure Draft.

The first case concerned recognition and measurement issues related to a simple cash transaction, and the Board Members all agreed on its treatment. However, difficulties arose in the next cases, which concerned receivables and payables. Those Board Members who wanted to keep the status quo intact became reluctant to endorse any use of current values as preferable to original cost–based numbers in any circumstances. This reluctance progressed even to the point that Board Member Robert Morgan said that he preferred the face value of a receivable in every circumstance, even if the interest rate was unrealistic. In effect, Board Members were looking past the general concepts at the top to see what impact they would have on the specific practices that would be derived from them. This tendency (which became known as "peeking at the answers") was an example of the compromising between the prescriptive and descriptive approaches described earlier.

The deliberations became more and more difficult as the cases became more complex and closer to real issues in financial accounting. The "peeking" was clearly demonstrated in one case designed to have the Board Members address some issues related to how a savings and loan institution should account for its mortgage loans receivable. Several Board Members simply would not state their preference out of concern that the troubled savings and loan industry would interpret their hypothetical positions as an intent to modify practices then in use.

In the summer of 1982, it became clear that the Board Members were deeply divided on the most basic question: three (David Mosso, Robert Sprouse, and Ralph Walters) favored more use of current values than under the status quo; three (Frank Block, John March, and Robert Morgan) favored less use; and Don Kirk was somewhere in between. Furthermore, the members of the two main subgroups did not always see eye to eye on the reasons for their positions. At the end of the summer, those Board Members who favored keeping the status quo publicly voiced a worry that the Staff members were biased in favor of current values and were thus unable to offer legitimate assistance. In an effort to achieve some progress, two separate Staff teams were created and the Board engaged Dr. Robert K. Mautz as a consultant. Because he was reputed to be an advocate for maintaining the status quo, his engagement was seen by many as an attempt to counterbalance the presence of Dr. Sterling. Despite the ensuing efforts to seek a consensus, the Board remained at an impasse. The division held, even though there had been one change in the Board's membership—Vic Brown replaced Morgan, formerly of Caterpillar Tractor.

Later in 1983, the Board abandoned its original goal for the recognition and measurement phase in favor of another strategy that would allow the Board Members to agree on some issues and get a SFAC published. In order to do so, about the only choice was to draft a statement that would essentially endorse the previously published concepts and avoid coming to grips with the historical cost/current value question. Project managers Tim Lucas and Halsey Bullen (see page 48) were assigned to the project because Sterling's term of appointment was ending. Lucas was given the job because of the respect he had earned for his ability in forging a consensus on the difficult Pensions project. Even though he was just appointed to the staff, Bullen's assignment was supported because he was untainted by the previous events.

An Exposure Draft incorporating the chosen strategy was issued in December 1983, just before Ray Lauver replaced Ralph Walters as a Board Member. SFAC 5 was issued in December 1984, just before the replacement of Board Member John March by Art Wyatt. Although the statement does open some doors for change by including a new additional statement of comprehensive income and by acknowledging that current value information might be useful in some circumstances, the movement toward a descriptive framework prevents the statement from providing much prescriptive guidance.

Not-for-profit concepts. The final step in the Conceptual Framework project was an effort to develop concepts that would guide the Board and its constituents in dealing with accounting for entities other than business enterprises. At the time that SFAC 4 was completed, these entities were called *nonbusiness,* but the term was resented by their managers because it seemed to imply that they were not "businesslike." As a compromise, SFAC 6 uses the term *not-for-profit.*

There was substantial confusion at this stage in the project as to how to accomplish the extension of the Conceptual Framework to not-for-profit entities. SFAC 4 was comparable to SFAC 1, but did not repeat much of its content because the objectives of accounting for the two types of organizations are so different. However, there were no differences in the qualitative characteristics of useful information provided to statement users, and there were many similarities in the elements used in the financial statements issued by both types of entities. The process was further delayed by the stalemate in the recognition and measurement phase because of some similarities in the issues concerning the timing and amounts of revenues. Some fears also existed that opening SFAC 3 for amendment would bring about new debates from Board Members and constituents who found the original version to be oriented too strongly toward current values. The final decision was to issue SFAC 6 as an amendment to SFAC 3 that would add new elements but leave the old ones intact. Once SFAC 5 was issued, the way was cleared for the amendment, which was issued in December 1985.

Some Observations on the Events

As of 1987, enough time had passed to allow evaluations of the somewhat disappointing outcome of the recognition and measurement phase of the project, which was particularly meaningful in terms of the potential that existed for its contributions beyond the levels achieved by other authoritative efforts to define concepts. Four factors can be considered to be sources of the difficulties that were encountered.

The people. It is certainly possible that a different mix of Board and Staff members might have led to different results. In any political process, it is inevitable that personality factors will enter into the deliberations and affect the outcome. Perhaps if different people had been involved (with different experience, emotional makeups, and knowledge of concepts and the mental processes of conceptualization), a different resolution could have been achieved. Of course, it is also possible that a different set of people might have produced a less useful statement.

The process. Over the long life of the Conceptual Framework project, the FASB's due process underwent substantial change. The project started when Board deliberations were private, with the result that the constituents did not have much information about the proceedings before the publication of a document. Later, particularly in the recognition and measurement phase, Board Members felt that they were on public display and they found it very difficult to engage in open exchanges of ideas. They became cautious about even listening to another viewpoint or granting an assumption for the sake of argument because doing so might have been interpreted as a shift in their own position. Because the public discussion forced Board Members into inflexible attitudes, it became very difficult for them to find the common ground that is so essential to forging compromises and consensus.

Constituents. Throughout the Conceptual Framework project, the FASB received a consistent message from many of its constituents that the status quo should be preserved. Accordingly, tension increased whenever the Board's discussions seemed to suggest a change in practice. Because the constituents were so highly concerned, they became very active in the formal due process and in communicating informally through speeches and other media. For example, the proceedings in the project were the subject of discussions of the "Business Roundtable," a group comprised of the chief operating executives of the very largest corporations. Unavoidably, tension in the constituencies added to the uncertainty and division felt among the Board and Staff members and made compromise that much more difficult.

Balance of powers. Over the 12-year life of the project, some observers believe that there were some significant changes in how the Board obtains its authority, with the result that its ability to forge prescriptive concepts was constrained, eventually to the point that it could do nothing other than describe current practice.

The project began in 1973, when auditors (acting primarily through the AICPA) constituted the most influential constituent group. At this stage, the Board approached the Conceptual Framework project with the traditional strategy that reasonable people could come to intelligent conclusions through research and through careful and private deliberations.

The mid-1970s saw the profession and the Board facing new problems because of investigations conducted by Senator Lee Metcalf and Congressman John Moss. Even though legislation was not ever close to being enacted, the investigations and the publicity created by them did spur a number of reforms that reduced the AICPA's influence over the FASB and revived the SEC's use of the oversight powers it had been granted by the 1934 Securities Act.[5] Also at the time of the investigations, two powerful positions were occupied by persons who had a bent toward reform. The Chairman of the SEC was Harold Williams, an advocate of greater social responsibility for corporations. The Chief Accountant was Dr. John C. ("Sandy") Burton, an accounting professor who supported the presentation of more information based on current values. Evidence of the SEC's power over the FASB can be seen in its 1978 action rejecting the Board's carefully developed position in SFAS 19 on accounting by producers of oil and natural gas. This shift in power from auditors to users may have caused the Board to become more innovative, as characterized by the 1979 issuance of SFAS 33 that began the FASB's own requirements for current value disclosures. It was in this era that the ground work was laid for the first three Statements of Financial Accounting Concepts.

The beginning of the 1980s saw another change in the power structure with the election of President Ronald Reagan in an atmosphere that favored less regulation. Among his appointments was a new Chairman of the SEC, John S. R. Shad, who had a far less activist attitude than Harold Williams. After Burton's departure in 1976, the Chief Accountant's office was filled by Clarence Sampson, who had served on the SEC staff for a number of years prior to his appointment. He adopted a less visible profile than the one Burton established.

In effect, these changes created a vacuum of power for the FASB because the auditors' influence had been diminished and the SEC's involvement on behalf of users was reduced. To a certain extent, this void was filled by statement preparers, as represented by the Financial Executives Institute and individuals from specific corporations. They were able to use the FASB's due process procedures effectively, as shown in their success in having SFAS 8 (on foreign currency translation) repealed and replaced by SFAS 52, which they generally consider preferable. Preparers also became more dominant in

---

[5] See Mark Moran and Gary John Previts, "The SEC and the Profession, 1934–84: The Realities of Self-Regulation," *Journal of Accountancy,* July 1984, pp. 68–80.

the due process. Some indication of their involvement is provided by the responses to the defeasance Exposure Draft (Chapter 3 showed that over half of them came from preparers) and by the proportion of their donations to the Foundation (Chapter 2 showed that about half of the donations came from preparers). The potential problem created by such dominance by preparers is discussed at length in the Epilogue.

Without the clear mandate that it had in the second half of the 1970s to move ahead with a prescriptive framework that might imply major reforms, the Board has apparently backed off in the 1980s to a less active stance and has adopted a more defensive position on the question of whether it is an institution of reform. In 1983, for example, Dr. Paul Pacter, then the Executive Director of the Financial Accounting Foundation, included this statement in his article in the *Journal of Accountancy:*

> ...all board members agree on one major point: if any significant change is ultimately concluded to be necessary, the change must be accomplished through a gradual, evolutionary process.[6]

SFAC 5 officially repeats the same defensive idea with this comment in paragraph 2:

> The recognition criteria and guidance in this Statement are generally consistent with current practice and do not imply radical change. Nor do they foreclose the possibility of future changes in practice. The Board intends future change to occur in the gradual, evolutionary way that has characterized past change.

This posture was also assumed in SFAS 87, which represented a significant withdrawal from the position expressed in the 1982 Preliminary Views discussion document. The following paragraph explained the Board's justification for the compromise that it reached:

> After considering the range of comments on *Preliminary Views* and the Exposure draft, the Board concluded that the changes required by this Statement represent a worthwhile improvement in financial reporting. Opinion 8 noted in 1966 that "accounting for pensions cost is in a transitional stage" (paragraph 17). The Board believes that is still true in 1985. FASB Concepts Statement No. 5, *Recognition and Measurement in Financial Statements of Business Enterprises,* indicates that "the Board intends future change [in practice] to occur in the gradual, evolutionary way that has characterized past change." The Board realizes that the evolutionary change in some areas may have to be slower than in others. The Board believes that it would be conceptually appropriate and preferable to recognize a net pension liability or asset measured as the difference between the projected benefit obligation and plan assets, either with no delay in recognition of gains or losses, or perhaps with gains and losses reported currently in comprehensive income but not in earnings. However, it concluded that that

---

[6]Paul A. Pacter, "The Conceptual Framework: Make No Mystique about It," *Journal of Accountancy,* July 1983, p. 86.

approach would be too great a change from current practice to be adopted at the present time. In light of the differences in respondents' views and the practical considerations noted, the Board concluded that the provisions of this Statement as a whole represent an improvement in financial reporting.[7]

A careful study of this rather lengthy quote shows a number of points; for the immediate purpose, attention should be focused on the declaration by the Board Members that they *know* that the answer in the standard is not best but they are willing to require it because it is (1) a slight improvement and (2) acceptable to the constituents. In the authors' opinion, this position represents an unambiguous abandonment of the prescriptive nature of the Conceptual Framework.

Summary

The authors conclude that the FASB's Conceptual Framework project did not achieve its original goals. Apparently, at least some Board Members also acknowledged that the project would not accomplish all that it was thought that it could achieve because these comments were included in the introduction to the Exposure Draft that eventually became SFAC 5:

> This process [of dealing with recognition and measurement questions] may have raised hopes that the Board's concepts Statements on recognition and measurement would produce instant, indisputable answers to questions about whether a particular event should be recognized and when, and what amount best measures it.
>
> If so, those were false hopes. . . . concepts are tools for solving problems.

These comments can be interpreted to be the Board's denial of its ability to produce prescriptive concepts that would allow practicing accountants to solve problems without a published standard. In effect, this quote says that authoritative guidance will be necessary.

As an interesting anecdote, the authors of a journal article on financial reporting attempted to apply SFAC 5 to resolve an issue concerning a new type of financial instrument, but could only conclude that:

> Unfortunately, none of these [concepts] provide guidance in resolving [the issues at hand]. . . . It seems necessary for these [recognition and measurement conceptual] issues to be resolved, or at least addressed more fully, before the definitions of the elements of financial statements [in SFAC 3] can be made operational.[8]

In summary, as a result of the changes in the Conceptual Framework project (for whatever reasons they came about), the resulting framework is

---

[7]"Employers' Accounting for Pensions," Statement of Financial Accounting Standards No. 87, par. 103.

[8]Richard L. Rogers and Krishnagopal Menon, "Accounting for Deferred-Payment Notes," *The Accounting Review*, July 1985, p. 555.

neither very **prescriptive** nor very **descriptive**. By the Board's own admission in the Exposure Draft and in the paragraph on the use of different measurement attributes in practice (see page 116), the Conceptual Framework does not provide operational guidance. Furthermore, it is not sufficiently descriptive to be useful for explaining to nonaccountants just exactly what it is that accountants do. For example, the statement of comprehensive income described in SFAC 5 is not presented by any corporations.

It is perhaps an overstatement to call the project a failure, although it is certainly a disappointment to many. On the other hand, it makes a positive contribution to the accounting literature by establishing service to user needs as the primary objective of financial accounting. It also has contributed to the efficiency of the due process procedures by defining a number of key terms that are indeed used by the Board and its constituents. These accomplishments may bring more rigor and efficiency to the Board's deliberations, but that conclusion can be safely reached only in the long run, particularly as the Board Members who created the framework are replaced by others who had no part in its development.

Any conclusion as to whether the project was worth the effort is highly subjective and depends on what was wanted out of the project and the assessment of what was obtained. In the authors' opinions, it seems to have been an appropriate use of resources and there are more benefits to be obtained from it.

A SUMMARY AND EVALUATION OF THE CONTENTS OF THE CONCEPTS STATEMENTS

This section briefly summarizes the basic points in the Statements of Financial Accounting Concepts issued by the FASB as part of its Conceptual Framework project. More detailed descriptions are beyond the scope of this book; however, they can be found in most Accounting Theory textbooks. In addition to describing the contents of the Statements, this section includes commentaries on the political nature of the Board and its activities.

Statement of Financial Accounting Concepts No. 1: Objectives of Financial Reporting by Business Enterprises

As mentioned briefly in an earlier part of the chapter, the foundation for SFAC 1 was the work of the AICPA's Trueblood Study Group on the Objectives of Financial Statements. Discussion Memoranda related to the topic were published by the Board in 1974 and 1976, and its Exposure Draft was distributed in 1977. The Statement was released in 1978.

The overall purpose of SFAC 1 is to state the highest level concepts in the prescriptive top-down structure adopted by the FASB. In doing so, the Board identified the primary objective for financial reporting and then clarified it with several others. The overriding primary objective was stated as follows:

> Financial reporting should provide information that is useful to present and potential investors and creditors and other users in making rational investment, credit, and similar decisions. (par. 34)

By establishing this objective, the Statement elevates users to the highest level of priority among the Board's constituents. Pursuing this objective requires that all new and existing generally accepted accounting principles be evaluated in terms of their contribution to the usefulness of the information provided to investors, creditors, and other decision makers whose position external to the organization limits their access to financial data.

To bring this very high-level objective down to a more applicable level, the Board went on to clarify it with these two subobjectives:

> Financial reporting should provide information to help present and potential investors and creditors and other users in assessing the amounts, timing, and uncertainty of prospective cash receipts from dividends or interest and the proceeds from the sale, redemption, or maturity of securities or loans. (par. 37)

> Financial reporting should provide information about the economic resources of an enterprise, the claims to those resources (obligations of the enterprise to transfer resources to other entities and owners' equity), and the effects of transactions, events, and circumstances that change resources and claims to those resources. (par. 40)

A notable additional feature of the Statement is its description of some of the qualities of the users that the Board said that it would be concerned with. Specifically, the Statement says:

> The information should be comprehensible to those who have a reasonable understanding of business and economic activities and are willing to study the information with reasonable diligence. (par. 34)

By creating this policy, the Board can usually disregard arguments that proposed information might not be understood by "typical" or "naive" investors. Although these people receive financial statements, the FASB does not intend to simplify the information to the point that it will be immediately comprehensible without training and effort. The policy is not an effort to make the statements complex but an acknowledgment that the complexity of statements arises from the complexity of the underlying economics.

Perhaps the greatest significance of SFAC 1 lies in its formalization on the **conceptual** level of the **political** fact that the Board has to put users' interests first because their needs are the source of the SEC's own mandate for setting accounting standards and thus critical to its endorsement of the FASB as the primary standards-setting body.

Statement of Financial Accounting Concepts No. 2: Qualitative Characteristics of Accounting Information

Some material on the qualities of useful information was included in the 1976 Discussion Memorandum on the Conceptual Framework project and the 1977 Exposure Draft that led to SFAC 1; however, some controversies caused the Board to omit material from SFAC 1 in order that the objectives could be published without additional debate. A second Exposure Draft was released in 1979, and SFAC 2 was issued in 1980.

The overall purpose of the Statement is to identify criteria for determining whether information is useful for decisions to be made by users of financial statements. If the information at issue has the qualities, it should be reported; if it does not have them, it should not be reported. In accomplishing this goal, the Board identified a hierarchy of qualities of useful information.

Decision usefulness was selected as the most significant of these qualities because of the importance that the primary objective of SFAC 1 had assigned to users.

The Board went on to provide clarification by describing two primary qualities that produce decision usefulness. **Relevance** is defined in the Glossary to the Statement as "the capacity of information to make a difference in a decision . . ." The discussion explains that, in turn, relevance is imparted to information when it is available to the user with **timeliness**, and has either **predictive value** or **feedback value**, or **both**. In other words, relevant information must be able to help the user make better forecasts of the future or better evaluations of the past.

The second primary quality of useful information is **reliability**, which is defined in the Glossary to be "the quality . . . that assures that information is reasonably free from error and bias and faithfully represents what it purports to represent." In order to be reliable, the information must be subject to testing to assure that its preparation is legitimate and it must correspond to what it is thought to present. Additionally, the information is to be **neutral**, which is a quality imparted by standards setters. That is, they are not to attempt to use the system to achieve any goal other than better decisions by investors, creditors, and others. For example, a proposed standard for accounting by banks might more closely represent the risks in that industry, with the result that the amounts of their reported profits would be drastically changed. The possibility that the change might speed up the failure of some banks or cause others to succeed should not be a factor in the decision if neutrality is to be obtained. Thus, including neutrality in the hierarchy was another situation in which the political nature of standards setting was captured in the concepts.

The Statement identified **comparability** as a secondary qualitative characteristic of useful information and defined it as "the quality . . . that enables users to identify similarities in and differences between two sets of economic phenomena." Some confusion exists between the meanings of comparability and **consistency**, which SFAC 2 defines as "conformity from period to period with unchanging policies and procedures." SFAC 2 makes the point that consistency is necessary to achieve comparability but is not sufficient (par. 117). A similar quality, **uniformity,** was not defined in SFAC 2. It is commonly considered to be the result of the use of the same policies and procedures by all reporting companies.

In addition to possessing these three qualities (relevance, reliability, and comparability), useful accounting information must pass a **materiality** threshold, such that the magnitude of the reported amount is large enough to affect decisions. Clearly, there is a relationship between materiality and relevance. In effect, the Board decided that relevance relates to the subject matter of the information, whereas materiality relates to the size of the amount reported. Drawing this distinction may create confusion because auditors and other accountants have tended to use the two terms synonymously.

Another test for decision usefulness described in SFAC 2 is the relationship between the **costs and benefits** of an item of information (pars. 133–44). In short, the Statement holds that information must produce benefits in excess of its costs in order to be useful. While that concept is not likely to be challenged philosophically, an argument can certainly be made that it has only a small chance of ever helping the Board reach a decision. For one thing, there are no unambiguous techniques for measuring the costs and benefits of information. For another, costs may be borne by some groups and benefits may be gained by others, and the decision that must be made is who is going to get how much of which. In most comment letters that appeal to this test, it is usually apparent that the respondents are arguing that **their** costs of complying with the proposed standard will exceed **their** benefits. It seems self-evident that this condition will exist for someone in every controversial situation. If everyone's benefits must exceed their own costs, then no standards-setting system would be needed because all parties would adopt the practice voluntarily. Indeed, it is the need to impose costs on some parties to the benefit of others that causes a political system to be created; there is no reason to expect the FASB's situation to be any different.

As an overall evaluation of SFAC 2, it provides a set of definitions that the Board and its constituents can and do use to communicate with each other. The definitions should bring more rigor to the due process, and possibly to the thought processes of the participants. They certainly provide enough leeway to allow different interpretations by different people, but at least they lend direction to the deliberations, and can be considered worthwhile for that reason alone.

Statement of Financial Accounting Concepts No. 3: Elements of Financial Statements of Business Enterprises

Some material about the elements was included in the 1977 Exposure Draft that led to SFAC 1, but, again because of controversy, it was carved out and placed in a different phase of the Conceptual Framework project. That work led to another Exposure Draft in 1979, with the final pronouncement coming out late in 1980.

The overall purpose of the statement is to identify and define the components from which financial statements are constructed. The term **elements** is defined in SFAC 3 as "the building blocks with which financial statements are constructed—the classes of items that financial statements comprise" (par. 5). Ten elements are defined, and a reference is made to the fact that the Board might define others later. The 10 elements are:

- Assets
- Liabilities
- Owners' equity
- Investments by owners
- Distributions to owners

- Comprehensive income
  - ☐ Revenues
  - ☐ Expenses
  - ☐ Gains
  - ☐ Losses

Assets and liabilities are the two most primary elements because the definitions of the other eight are based on them. For example, revenues are defined as "inflows or other enhancements of assets of an entity or settlements of its liabilities (or a combination of both) during a period" (par. 63).

Despite the familiarity of the terms and the simplicity of their definitions, SFAC 3 sparked controversy among some accountants, particularly those who want to preserve the status quo. Specifically, they see the emphasis on assets and liabilities as an abandonment of the traditional preference for the income statement that has existed for decades in standards setting. A familiar example of a preference for the income statement is the use of LIFO inventory measures. In most cases, the preference for LIFO is justified on the basis that it produces a desirable measure of the cost of goods sold (and, thereby, net income), despite the fact that the number reported for the inventory on the statement of financial position does not reflect either the current value or the actual purchase price of the goods on hand. The apparent movement in SFAC 3 toward equalization of the income statement and the statement of financial position represents a change from current practice that particularly alarms those who desire maintenance of the status quo.

As mentioned earlier, the use of the concepts of "comprehensive income" instead of "earnings" or "net income" also proved controversial, because it seemed to portend a shift to more current value information.

The authors' evaluation of SFAC 3 is not unlike their evaluation of SFAC 2. The Statement defines some commonly used terms, and thus has added to the rigor and efficiency of the communications portion of the due process; however, the definitions are subject to ambiguous interpretations and have not been operational.

Statement of Financial Accounting Concepts No. 4: Objectives of Reporting by Nonbusiness Organizations

The Report of the Trueblood Study Group included some objectives for financial statements issued by nonbusiness organizations. Rather than include them in SFAC 1, the Board set them aside at the beginning of the Conceptual Framework project to focus on business situations. In 1977, efforts to include them began, and a Discussion Memorandum was published in 1978. It was followed by hearings, and an Exposure Draft was released in March 1980. The final Statement was issued in December 1980.

The scope of the Statement does not include governmental entities because of political difficulties in obtaining support from that constituency. As mentioned earlier in the book, authority for setting standards in this area has been granted to the Governmental Accounting Standards Board.

Nonbusiness organizations are identified in paragraph 6 of the Statement as those entities that have the following three qualities:

- receipts of significant amounts of resources from resource providers who do not expect to receive either repayment or economic benefits proportionate to resources provided,
- operating purposes that are primarily other than to provide goods or services at a profit or profit equivalent, and
- absence of defined ownership interests that can be sold, transferred, or redeemed, or that convey entitlement to a share of a residual distribution of resources in the event of liquidation of the organization.

In other words, there are no owners, no profits, and no owners' equity in the same sense as they exist for a business.

The Statement identifies seven objectives of different levels of importance, and they are similar to the objectives established in SFAC 1 for business enterprises. For example, the first one holds that:

Financial reporting by nonbusiness organizations should provide information that is useful to present and potential resource providers and other users in making rational decisions about the allocation of resources to those organizations. (par. 35)

As clarification of this objective, SFAC 4 goes on to say that financial reporting for these organizations should provide information that will help statement users in:

...assessing the services that a nonbusiness organization provides and its ability to continue to provide those services. (par. 38)

...assessing how managers of a nonbusiness organization have discharged their stewardship responsibilities and about other aspects of their performance. (par. 40)

In meeting these objectives, the financial statements should provide information that is:

> about the economic resources, obligations, and net resources of an organization, and the effects of transactions, events, and circumstances that change resources and interests in those resources. (par. 43)

The authors' evaluation of SFAC 4 is actually directed at the nonbusiness phase of the project, which has proven to be less controversial than the other phases. Nonetheless, the nonbusiness issues have been difficult to resolve, primarily because the Board lacks a clear-cut mandate from the SEC or any other authoritative group to actually resolve them. Because substantial benefits have not flowed from this phase of the project, it is quite possible that the Board would be better off if it had never undertaken it.

Statement of Financial Accounting Concepts No. 5: Recognition and Measurement in Financial Statements of Business Enterprises

The procedural history and many of the political considerations associated with this phase of the project are described earlier in the chapter and will not be repeated here.

There were two conceptual goals for SFAC 5: the description of the basic set of financial statements and the description of **recognition criteria**, which are tests to determine whether and when information should be incorporated in the financial statements. The concepts of recognition are focused on the contents of the financial statements and do not apply to the additional disclosures included under the more inclusive area of financial reporting described in SFAC 1.

The section of SFAC 5 that describes the financial statements generally endorses the status quo, with the exception of its introduction of a second type of income statement. The five statements are listed below, together with a brief comment on each:

- **Statement of financial position.** The description suggests nothing particularly different from accepted practices.
- **Statement of earnings.** This statement would be essentially the same as the traditional income statement, except that it would *not* include cumulative effects of changes in accounting principles. The concept of this statement was created in order to alleviate concerns that the Board was going to discard traditional matching-based income measures.
- **Statement of comprehensive income.** No such statement currently exists in practice. It was included in SFAC 5 as a concession to those Board Members and constituents who wanted the Conceptual Framework to endorse a greater use of current values. By its presence in the concepts statement, their position is acknowledged, but no effect is

likely to be felt on practice for a long time, especially in light of the Board's decision in SFAS 89 to abandon the SFAS 33 experiment.

- **Statement of cash flows.** This statement is significantly different from the traditional statement of changes of financial position created by APBO 19 in 1971. According to the Board's 1986 Exposure Draft concerning the cash flow statement, it focuses on those events that caused cash and cash equivalents to come in and flow out of the enterprise, and categorizes them by their nature as either operating, financing, or investing. The goal is to provide a simple summary of what happened to the cash account. This information should allow statement users to more meaningfully assess their own cash flows from their investments.

- **Statement of investments by and distributions to owners.** This statement also exists only in concept, but it roughly corresponds to the traditional statement of changes in owners' equity. It would differ from that statement because it would not include any changes from income events. This difference comes about because of the decision to create two concepts of reported income and because of the Board's inability to construct a consensus in favor of either earnings or comprehensive income.

From the discussion earlier in the chapter and from the above comments, it can be seen that SFAC 5 was so greatly affected by political difficulties that compromises had to enter even into otherwise straightforward ideas of what type of information should be reported in which financial statement.

In describing the **recognition criteria**, the Board merely restated what it had said in the previous concepts statements; it identified the following four criteria in paragraph 63:

- *Definitions* The item [to be considered for recognition] meets the definition of an element of financial statements.
- *Measurability* It has a relevant attribute measurable with sufficient reliability.
- *Relevance* The information about it is capable of making a difference in user decisions.
- *Reliability* The information is representationally faithful, verifiable, and neutral.

Thus, after abandoning the initial strategy of issuing a concepts statement that would resolve substantive recognition issues and adopting the new strategy of issuing a statement that a significant majority of Board Members would endorse,[9] essentially all that could be accomplished was to repeat what had been said in SFAC 2 and SFAC 3. The entire content of the recognition

---

[9]John March's dissent to SFAC 5 was the only negative vote cast by any Board Member on any of the six concepts statements.

criteria can be summarized as follows: If relevant and reliable quantitative financial information is available about an item, it should be included in the financial statements.

Furthermore, the last two criteria (relevance and reliability) are redundant—they merely repeat the meaning of the second (measurability). The explanation for this duplication lies in the simple fact that it was necessary in order to get the six assenting Board Members to vote for SFAC 5.

The criteria also are too broad to provide helpful guidance either to standards setters or to individual accountants who are attempting to resolve a new issue. Again, the reason for this outcome is that the deep divisions among the Board Members could be overcome only by returning to high-level and basically unarguable generalities.

Statement of Financial Accounting Concepts No. 6: Elements of Financial Statements

SFAC 6 does not constitute a substantial modification of SFAC 3; rather, it is best viewed as an augmentation of the original pronouncement to make it applicable to what are now known as "not-for-profit" entities.

One difference is the substitution of the element **net assets** for owners' equity in order to deal with organizations that do not have either owners or equity in the traditional sense of the words.

The biggest difference is the identification of what are called "classes" of net assets for not-for-profit organizations. These components are not at the same level as the elements, but are nonetheless basic. They are: restricted net assets, temporarily restricted net assets, and unrestricted net assets. The first class identifies amounts that cannot be spent or used for any purpose inconsistent with the stipulations implied or otherwise established by an agreement between the entity and the donor of assets. For example, an endowment of a professorship will generally restrict the use of the donated and earned assets to compensation and other support of a faculty member. The second class encompasses those situations in which a restriction is placed on the use of the assets, but it will be removed by the passage of time or some other event. For example, a donor may endow a museum with a sum of money, with the understanding that the income will be used during the donor's lifetime to acquire certain types of art; at the donor's death, the restriction will be lifted, and the funds can be used as needed for any purpose. The third class refers to those funds that can be used for whatever purpose the management of the entity decides.

The Board has not had much opportunity to deal with these extensions of the elements, with the result that it is hard to determine whether they are indeed useful. In general, the effects of the amendments to SFAC 3 will not be felt by most accountants and users.

SELECTED READINGS

DOPUCH, NICHOLAS, and SHYAM SUNDER. "FASB's Statement on Objectives and Elements of Financial Accounting: A Review." *The Accounting Review,* January 1980, pp. 1–21.

MILLER, PAUL B. W. "The Conceptual Framework: Myths and Realities." *Journal of Accountancy,* March 1985, pp. 62–71.

PACTER, PAUL A. "The Conceptual Framework: Make No Mystique about It." *Journal of Accountancy,* July 1983, pp. 76–88.

SOLOMONS, DAVID. "The FASB's Conceptual Framework: An Evaluation." *Journal of Accountancy,* June 1986, pp. 114–24.

SPROUSE, ROBERT T. "The Importance of Earnings in the Conceptual Framework." *Journal of Accountancy,* January 1978, pp. 64–71.

REVIEW QUESTIONS

1. Why is the FASB's Conceptual Framework considered important?

2. List three general reasons for developing a conceptual framework.

3. What is one main goal of a descriptive conceptual framework?

4. Why is a descriptive framework also called "bottom-up"?

5. Describe the advantages and disadvantages of a descriptive framework.

6. Explain why a descriptive framework often does not provide guidance to a standards-setting body like the FASB.

7. What is one main goal of a prescriptive conceptual framework?

8. Why is a prescriptive framework also called "top-down"?

9. Describe the advantages and disadvantages of a prescriptive framework.

10. Explain why it is difficult for an authoritative body to establish a prescriptive framework.

11. What are two advantages of having a conceptual framework that defines commonly used terms?

12. What difficulty is encountered in applying definitions that are part of a conceptual framework?

13. What are three objectives of the FASB's Conceptual Framework? Was the framework intended to be prescriptive or descriptive?

14. Many accountants would prefer to leave the status quo intact. Is this preference unique to accountants? What difficulty does it tend to cause in efforts to produce a conceptual framework?

15. What did the FASB state in Statement of Financial Accounting Concepts No. 5 that shows that the Conceptual Framework is at least partially descriptive?

16. Identify the broad accounting issues that were originally established for the "recognition and measurement" phase of the Conceptual Framework project. What other controversial issue seemed to draw the most attention?

17. What action is described as "peeking," and why did it interfere with the development of the Conceptual Framework?

18. Why would it be important to issue a Statement of Financial Accounting Concepts (or any other pronouncement based on a consensus) *before* a Board Member was replaced after the end of his or her term?

19. Why did an open due process make it difficult to develop the Conceptual Framework? Despite this problem, why was it considered essential to have one?

20. Describe the shifts in the "balance of powers" that occurred during the life of the Conceptual Framework project.

21. The March 22, 1985, Exposure Draft on pensions includes a paragraph in which the Board Members describe their real preference and the reasons why they were not proposing a standard consistent with that preference. Discuss the implications of this paragraph for the Board's ability to resolve issues.

22. What are the two major contributions of the FASB's Conceptual Framework?

23. How many Statements of Financial Accounting Concepts were issued by the FASB through the fall of 1985? What are their titles?

24. According to SFAC 1, what is the primary objective of financial reporting? What is the political significance of this objective?

25. What type of financial statement user did the FASB identify as being most important? Why is this choice significant?

26. According to SFAC 2, what are the two "primary" qualities of useful information?

27. Why is there little guidance in a policy that states that the benefits of providing information should exceed its costs?

28. Identify the 10 elements of financial statements defined in SFAC 3. Which two are the most "primary"? Why might this status of these elements be considered "revolutionary"?

29. List some examples of "nonbusiness" organizations. Why have nonbusiness accounting issues been difficult for the FASB to resolve?

30. Identify the five financial statements described in SFAC 5. Explain the difference between the two types of income statements.

31. List the four recognition criteria defined in SFAC 5. How do they repeat SFAC 2? Why are two of these criteria redundant?

32. What is the primary modification that SFAC 6 makes to SFAC 3?

33. What term does SFAC 6 use to describe the element equivalent to owners' equity for not-for-profit organizations?

34. List the classes of net assets of not-for-profit organizations identified in SFAC 6.

EXERCISES

1. There is a difference between descriptive and prescriptive approaches to developing a theory. Use these approaches to describe the way an activity is carried out at your school and to prescribe the way you think it should be carried out. For

example, you might select the registration process, the allocation of parking, the allocation of sports tickets, the granting of tenure, or the scheduling of placement interviews.

2. Suggest at least two broad objectives for financial accounting other than the one selected by the FASB. Discuss the implications of these alternative objectives for resolving accounting issues.

3. One alternative to accounting for assets on the balance sheet would be to report them at some measurement of their current value. Identify the parties you think would participate in the FASB's due process and why they would participate if the following assets were to be reported at current values:

   a. For agricultural products only.

   b. For assets of manufacturing companies only.

   c. For all assets.

4. The text identified *A Statement of Basic Accounting Theory* as a top-down (prescriptive) framework for financial accounting published by the American Accounting Association. Obtain a copy of this publication, perhaps from your library, and describe the resolution of the issue on whether financial statements would be based on historical costs or current values.

EPILOGUE

A Look into the FASB's Future

The preceding chapters have shown how the Financial Accounting Standards Board works toward its overall goal of improving the practice of financial accounting. In doing so, the book has described the **people**, the **process**, and the **politics** of the FASB and has provided some insights into the **history** of standards setting. At this point, it is appropriate to look ahead to the **future** of the Board and to examine the factors that are likely to affect its ability to keep operating. The following issues are discussed:

- Public versus private standards setting
- Standards overload versus timely guidance
- Statement preparer participation versus dominance

In addition, there is an overall evaluation of the outlook for the FASB's future.

PUBLIC VERSUS PRIVATE STANDARDS SETTING

Throughout the 50-year history of financial accounting standards setting, there have been many debates whether the process should be carried out in the **public** sector of the economy or within the **private** sector. In most cases, the consensus has been that it is far more preferable to have it within the private sector.

In one sense, this issue may no longer be worth debating because the process is already very much in the public sector. The preceding chapters have shown that the FASB's due process procedures allow all participants to express their beliefs on the questions before it. The Board is designed to be independent of each of them while being dependent on all of them. Furthermore (and very important), the primary sources of the FASB's authority are the endorsements of its standards by the Securities and Exchange Commission and by state boards of public accountancy.

Thus, the issue might be better stated as whether the SEC should have **direct** responsibility for this public standards-setting process instead of merely having a position of "oversight." In evaluating the issue, it is helpful to determine what the SEC gains by having the FASB in operation.

First, **accounting standards are being established**. Controversial issues are debated at the FASB and many of them are eventually resolved, with the result that the SEC has the guidance it needs.

Second, **the SEC is able to influence the FASB's agenda**. Thus, the Commission is able to have its most urgent issues resolved when it needs guidance.

Third, **the SEC is potentially able to influence the outcome** of the process through its authority to establish its own rules for its registrants if it disagrees with the FASB. This ability is exercised through the SEC's formal and informal communication of its desires to the FASB described in Chapter 4. The ultimate threat of a "veto" (like the one exercised on SFAS 19, "Financial Accounting and Reporting by Oil and Gas Producing Companies") is always there to help assure that the Board remains conscious of its need to satisfy the SEC.

Fourth, the arrangement **allows the SEC to shift critics' attention from itself to the FASB**. By passing issues along to the Board for resolution, the heat of public scrutiny is focused on the Board and taken off the Commission, which has a lot of other controversial tasks to accomplish. This ability to direct attention to the FASB was described in the Prologue for the defeasance project. When the problem emerged, the SEC placed a moratorium on the recognition of gains from defeasance transactions and then sat back and waited for the Board to resolve the issues.

Fifth, **the SEC does not have to bear many costs of the process**. None of the Financial Accounting Foundation's funds for the FASB's budget come from the SEC or any other government agency. In effect, the only costs the SEC incurs are related to communications with the Board and occasional transportation costs to enable its personnel to observe and participate in various meetings.

Sixth, **the SEC obtains the services of many people who might not be willing to work under government salary scales**. For example, SEC Commissioners are paid only $77,500 annually, in contrast to the $240,000 paid to FASB Members. The SEC's Chief Accountant earns $77,500 per year, while the FASB's Director of Research makes $240,000. The salaries of the Chief Accountant's staff members range between $45,000 and $70,000, whereas FASB Project Managers earn between $65,000 and $105,000. Although working at the SEC may provide an intangible benefit from performing a public service, it seems unlikely that the Commission would be able to consistently locate, hire, and retain people whose talents and backgrounds are equal to those of the people at the FASB and who are willing to make a long-term commitment.

Given these six advantages of the present system, the SEC is unlikely to voluntarily assume full responsibility for the tasks that the FASB accomplishes. Thus, any motivation for the government to take over the job will probably have to come from outside the Commission. In turn, that development can happen only through a strong consensus in Congress that something is wrong with standards setting and that it can be remedied only by direct government control. Furthermore, that consensus can be developed only if events occur that raise sufficiently high concerns in Congress to cause the issue to rank above other problems that currently have a higher priority, such as the reduction of the deficit, tax reform, defense spending, foreign relations, and critical local issues that affect the chances of reelection.

A potential source of heightened congressional interest in standards setting might be the financial failure of large numbers of banks or major corporations that significantly injure or inconvenience a large number of voters. Even then, it would be necessary to draw a strong connection between these ill effects and financial accounting standards, *and* to demonstrate that having standards setting take place outside the direct responsibility of the SEC significantly contributes to the problem. Finally, it would have to be shown that putting the process directly under the SEC would create lower costs than modifying the existing process to eliminate its shortcomings.

In conclusion, it seems extremely unlikely that the FASB will be disbanded in favor of a system subject to direct governmental control. Of course, there are degrees of control over the FASB that the SEC might exert, such as a more visible involvement in the due process, representation on the Board of Trustees, and partial funding of the Board's budget. At present, however, there does not appear to be much impetus for even these steps to occur.

Congressional Attention

As described briefly in Chapter 5, congressional investigations in the mid-1970s called attention to the accounting profession and the FASB. The primary leaders were Senator Lee Metcalf of Montana and Congressman John Moss of California. Their subcommittees examined a number of issues, and some changes were made in 1977 as a result of the investigation. For example, the FASB's due process procedures were opened to more observation and public participation. The AICPA's influence on the Financial Accounting Foundation and the FASB was significantly reduced. The AICPA also went through a restructuring that distinguished between those members whose clients include SEC registrants and those whose clients are not registrants. However, hindsight has shown that there was no real possibility that any legislation could have been passed, possibly because of the reforms that were instituted, but more likely because neither Metcalf nor Moss was able to generate enough enthusiasm among his colleagues to raise the priority of the issues sufficiently high to cause them to pass new laws.

Beginning in 1985, congressional attention was again focused on the public accounting profession as a result of an investigation conducted by Congressman John Dingell (of Michigan) through his Oversight and Investigations Subcommittee of the House Committee on Energy and Commerce. One issue initially pursued by the subcommittee was the question of whether the existing standards-setting process shares any of the blame for a number of business failures that had inconvenienced many depositors of banks and savings and loan associations. Among those testifying at the first session of the hearings was FASB Chairman Don Kirk. Although that session of the hearings directed some attention to the standards-setting process, the FASB quickly passed from the center of attention as it became apparent that there was no clear link between its activities and the problems that had been encountered.

In the summer of 1987, it did not appear that there would be any legislative or other significant pressure to move the FASB's activities directly under government responsibility. However, it is always possible that attention directed at the SEC will increase the intensity of its participation in the Board's due process.

STANDARDS OVERLOAD VERSUS TIMELY GUIDANCE

Like other regulatory institutions, the FASB has to tread a fine line between doing too much and doing too little in its standards setting. If it does too much, it takes away the flexibility and judgment that allow accountants to cope with the specific situations they encounter in describing different companies in different industries. The presence of too many standards also makes practicing accountants learn new material, with the result that their costs increase, both in terms of educating themselves and in the risks that they face for practicing without being up to date.

On the other hand, doing too little creates the problem of excessive flexibility, such that the desired uniformity and comparability can be lost. This flexibility also increases the likelihood that some managers and auditors could more easily abuse the system. Additionally, having too little guidance might make it more difficult for other auditors to stand up to strong clients who are trying to push the standards to their limits or take advantage of loopholes in the standards.

Another factor the Board must consider is the interaction among its sources of authority. Exhibit E–1 illustrates a significant conflict that arises because the different organizations that have endorsed the FASB have authority over different parties. Specifically, the Board gets authority from the SEC to establish many of the standards used by registrants in their filings with the Commission. These companies are larger, their securities are usually widely held and actively traded, and their financial reports are widely distributed

EXHIBIT E–1 Conflicts between the Sources of the FASB's Authority

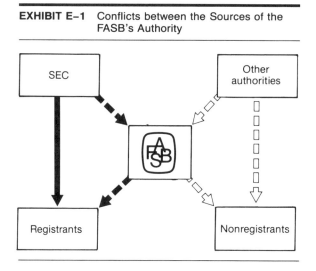

among investors and creditors. They are more likely to engage in complex transactions and have large and sophisticated accounting staffs that can implement new standards fairly easily. Furthermore, many of them are audited by major auditing firms that also have more sophisticated personnel.

The FASB also gets authority from State Boards of Public Accountancy and the AICPA. These organizations have authority over both SEC registrants and nonregistrants through the control that they can exert over independent auditors. The auditors of nonregistrant companies often have smaller practices and tend to be less sophisticated. Nonregistrants engage in fewer complex transactions, distribute their reports far less widely, and have smaller accounting staffs who are less capable of implementing new standards.

These differences between registrants and nonregistrants create a **dilemma** for the FASB. If the Board deals only with the SEC's needs in regulating registrants, it will tend to produce complex standards that are too sophisticated for the needs of nonregistrants and strain the abilities of the nonregistrants' accountants. But, if the FASB pays too much attention to the limitations of nonregistrants, its standards will not meet the SEC's needs and its authority will be jeopardized.

Standards Overload

Many observers seem to believe that the FASB has indeed issued too many standards or has focused too narrowly on SEC problems to the detriment of the needs of nonregistrants. To these people, there is a problem of **standards overload.**

EXHIBIT E-2 Pronouncements Published by the FASB

Year	Statements of Financial Accounting Standards	Interpre- tations	Statements of Financial Accounting Concepts	Technical Bulletins	Total
1973	1	0	0	0	1
1974	2	3	0	0	5
1975	9	4	0	0	13
1976	2	8	0	0	10
1977	6	5	0	0	11
1978	4	8	1	0	13
1979	10	2	0	19	31
1980	10	3	3	2	18
1981	9	3	0	6	18
1982	18	0	0	2	20
1983	7	1	0	0	8
1984	4	1	1	4	10
1985	6	0	1	6	13
1986	3	0	0	2	5
Total	91	38	6	41	176

As a crude sort of evidence, many critics have pointed to the high level of the Board's output in the late 1970s and early 1980s. To illustrate the grounds for this complaint, Exhibit E-2 shows the number of each of the four types of pronouncements that the FASB produced in each complete year of its life since 1973. Exhibit E-3 on page 142 presents the same data in graphical form. The Board apparently started slowly as it was getting established but then moved into a faster pace for 1979 through 1982. The total figure for 1979 is distorted by the large quantity of Technical Bulletins issued. Chapter 3 explains that this burst of output includes the answers to constituents' questions from earlier years that could not be published before Technical Bulletins were created in 1979. Subsequently, the level of output subsided.

But it is not enough to look merely at the **quantity** of output. Other critics have criticized the **specialized** nature of the standards as weakening the apparent significance of all standards. Examples of standards that might be overly specialized include SFAS 31, "Accounting for Tax Benefits Related to U. K. Tax Legislation concerning Stock Relief"; SFAS 44, "Accounting for Intangible Assets of Motor Carriers"; and SFAS 73, "Reporting a Change in Accounting for Railroad Track Structures." Because many of the standards produced in 1979–82 were either highly specialized like these, or extracted from AICPA publications to make the practices officially generally accepted, the numbers can be misleading. By the authors' reckoning, the level of output of significant and broadly applicable standards is substantially lower. The graph in Exhibit E-4 shows that, on the average, fewer than three significant standards have been issued each year, with as many as seven in only two years. This pattern is far different from the one depicted in Exhibit E-3, and

EXHIBIT E–3 Pronouncements Published by the FASB

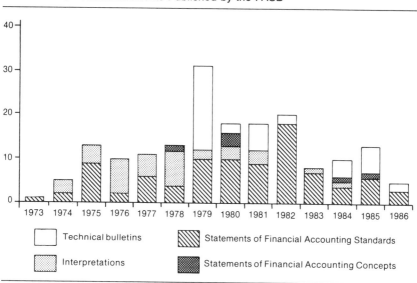

may serve to defuse some of the criticism that has been aimed at the Board for its high volume.

Still others have disparaged the Board for specifying **detailed procedures** instead of providing broader guidance that can be interpreted and applied by accountants and auditors who are closer to specific problems. As examples, they point to SFAS 13, "Accounting for Leases," and the many later pronouncements that were issued to modify and interpret its rules; SFAS 35, "Accounting and Reporting by Defined Benefit Pension Plans"; and SFAS 66, "Accounting for Sales of Real Estate." This criticism was also heard in the Board's deliberations and was documented in one Board member's dissent to SFAS 66, which begins with these words: "Mr. [Ralph] Walters dissents to the issuance of this Statement because he objects to incorporating these complex, rigid, and detailed rules into accounting standards."

At a relatively high philosophical level, there is no problem accepting the idea that an overload condition can be created. However, it is just as certain that people will disagree as to whether enough accountants have been sufficiently overloaded to justify a slowing or other change in the Board's level of activity. In evaluating this question, some insight may be gained in looking at other fields. For example, doctors usually do not complain that drug companies are producing too many new kinds of drugs. Rather, they tend to want all the different drugs that they can use to relieve their patients' discomfort. Similarly, ambitious auto mechanics generally do not demand that manufac-

EXHIBIT E–4 Significant Standards Issued by the FASB

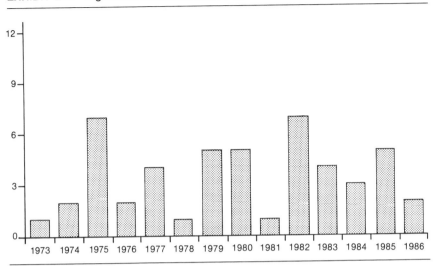

turers quit applying new technologies in designing cars. Instead, they simply learn how to service the new products to gain a competitive advantage over others who are less adaptable. It would also be an unfamiliar situation to find top tax accountants complaining to Congress about the complexity of the tax laws. Even if they do complain, they still keep learning the new laws to serve their clients and earn more fees.

On the other hand, complaints of a condition similar to standards overload have been heard from the managers of companies that have had to comply with the Occupational and Safety Health Act (OSHA) or the reporting requirements of the Employees' Retirement Income Security Act (ERISA).

Consequently, there is no simple answer to the question of whether overload has been reached for financial accounting. Because of their limited resources, companies that are not SEC registrants (and their auditors) are more likely to argue that they are overloaded than registrants and their auditors. Of course, some managements of SEC registrants are likely to complain of overload because they generally prefer less regulation to more, and because they prefer the flexibility provided by the status quo to the restrictions created by a new standard.

Timely Guidance

For those accountants and other observers who believe that the FASB has not issued enough standards or has not acted with sufficient speed to resolve new issues, there exists the problem that has been called **timely guidance.**

In effect, these critics complain that the due process procedures take so long that the reporting and accounting problems are no longer important by the time standards are finally issued. For one example, they can point to the Defeasance project described earlier in the book; it lasted more than 15 months despite the need for an urgent solution. For another example, the Board took two years and two Exposure Drafts to issue SFAS 77, "Transfers of Receivables with Recourse." Without faster resolutions, the Board's critics argue, preparers and auditors are left without guidance for too long, and those who are so inclined are given an undesirable opportunity to abuse the existing standards and mislead statement users.

On the other side of this issue, it has been argued that speeding up the due process would undermine the credibility of the consensus that the Board Members finally reach. It is also argued that auditors should be sufficiently independent and intelligent to interpret the existing literature to resolve most reporting problems without relying on special pronouncements. For example, they might assert that the SEC or the auditors of the first companies to set up defeasance trusts could have determined what to do under the existing standards for extinguishment of debt. Their response to the potential problem of abuse by some managers or auditors holds that such abuse is an **ethical** problem that is not related to standards. Therefore, they argue, the problem is beyond the scope of the FASB's responsibility.

The FASB's Response

Regardless of their positions on these questions about standards overload and timely guidance, the Members of the FASB cannot afford to ignore these criticisms; indeed, the politics of the situation make it essential for the Board to acknowledge in some way its concern about the complaints.

One response would be an attempt to develop two distinct sets of accounting principles; a more complex set would apply to SEC registrants, while a simpler and less costly one would be used by nonregistrants. This approach has often been labeled "Other Comprehensive Basis of Accounting," or "OCBOA" for short.[1] It has also been described as "differential measurement."[2] It is known less formally as "Big GAAP versus Little GAAP."

The Board has applied a variation of this strategy in some of its standards by limiting their applicability. For example, SFAS 21 exempts "nonpublic companies" from the requirements of APB Opinion 15 (for earnings per share disclosures) and SFAS 14 (for reporting information about segments of a company). The Statement defines a nonpublic company as "an enterprise

---

[1]An evaluation of one such alternative basis is described in Barry P. Robbins, "Perspectives on Tax Basis Financial Statements," *Journal of Accountancy,* August 1985, pp. 89–100.

[2]See Rholan E. Larson and Thomas P. Kelley, "Differential Measurement in Accounting Standards: The Concept Makes Sense," *Journal of Accountancy,* November 1984, pp. 78–90.

other than one (a) whose debt or equity securities trade in a public market on a foreign or domestic stock exchange or in the over-the-counter market (including securities quoted only locally or regionally) or (b) that is required to file financial statements with the Securities and Exchange Commission" (par. 13). Similarly, the FASB eliminated a cost for most companies by requiring that SFAS 33, "Accounting for Changing Prices," be applied only to the largest public companies (about 1,500) that met specified size criteria.

A widespread application of this "Big GAAP/Little GAAP" approach would produce its own set of problems. For example, it would be necessary to deal with the transition that would have to occur when a company grew in size or otherwise had to adopt Big GAAP and abandon Little GAAP. It is also possible that statement users would have a lower level of confidence in Little GAAP statements because they would represent a low-cost compromise. As a result, any savings in accounting costs might be overshadowed by a higher cost of capital that would reflect the higher risk of less useful financial information.

Because of these difficulties (and the results of a survey[3]), the FASB has decided against pursuing a full differential measurement system as a solution to the standards overload problem. However, its Members have taken other steps to bring some relief. For example, the current Board seems less willing to place items on the agenda; there are not nearly as many projects on the 1987 agenda as there were in 1979 through 1982. Also, as described in Chapter 3, the Board has stated its intent to use Technical Bulletins more frequently to shorten the due process procedures for projects that are not likely to affect many companies. To help solve the timely guidance problem, the Board created the Emerging Issues Task Force (EITF) in 1984; its purposes and operations are discussed below.

The Emerging Issues Task Force

The specific impetus for the creation of the EITF was a recommendation from the Structure Committee of the Financial Accounting Foundation trustees. Because of its permanence, the EITF differs from other Task Forces created for the limited purpose of advising the FASB staff on a single project or related projects. It consists of 16 members, nine of whom are high-level technical experts from the largest auditing firms. Two members come from smaller CPA firms, and four others are statement preparers. The remaining member (and Chairman) is the FASB's Director of Research and Technical Activities. The meetings are also attended by the Assistant Director of RTA and one or more Board Members. Very significantly, the SEC's Chief Accountant attends each meeting and participates actively in the delibera-

---

[3]The results are included in the FASB's 1983 Research Report entitled *Financial Reporting by Private Companies: Analysis and Diagnosis.*

tions. Apart from his presence, there is no representation from the statement user constituency.

The basic purpose of the EITF is to identify new accounting and reporting issues related to new and different types of transactions. In debating these issues, the members try to reach a consensus; there are three possible outcomes of these debates:

- **A consensus[4] that a single treatment is preferred.** In these cases no further action is considered necessary. The Chief Accountant has stated that he will accept this type of consensus as authoritative support for practices to be used in financial reports filed with the SEC. As of November 1986, 62 of 131 issues addressed by the EITF had been resolved by this type of consensus.
- **No consensus on the best treatment but agreement that the problem is narrow.** In these cases, no additional deliberations or resolutions are needed, because the problem does not affect enough companies to make the effort worthwhile.
- **No consensus on the best treatment but agreement that the problem is important.** In these cases, it is determined that the problem merits attention from the FASB because of its potentially widespread occurrence and its significance. In dealing with the problem, the Board may choose to let the Staff issue a Technical Bulletin to solve the problem or it may decide to add a project to its agenda. As of November 1986, 18 of 131 issues fell into this category, and were resolved with eight Technical Bulletins and three Standards.

Even though the EITF has a high potential for allowing the Board to provide guidance more quickly, it has created some significant difficulties.

Perhaps the most important problem is the question of whether a Task Force can legitimately assume the role of an authoritative standards-setting body. Apart from the endorsement by the SEC, through its Chief Accountant, no other group has sanctioned the EITF as authoritative. Consequently, it is not settled whether a consensus among its members would apply to companies that are not SEC registrants. Eventually, it will be necessary to determine whether a consensus will be covered by the AICPA's Ethics Rule 203 and similar rules under state laws that require an auditor to comply with FASB pronouncements. In defense of the EITF's authoritative standing, Board Member Jim Leisenring (when he was Director of Research and Technical Activities and chairman of the Task Force) made the point that these types of issues are being resolved in a public forum with extensive participation from a variety of individuals. Before the EITF, the issues were resolved in private conferences that may have involved only an auditor and a client, and perhaps

---

[4]In general, a consensus is considered to exist when no more than two members of the EITF disagree with the proposed accounting.

the Chief Accountant of the SEC. In his view, the EITF brings more sunshine into the process than ever existed before.

If the profession formally or informally accepts the proposition that at least some decisions of the EITF define GAAP, a question arises concerning the proper medium for disseminating those decisions to the profession. To deal with this matter, it may be necessary to identify a new type of pronouncement that would be issued.

The minutes of the Task Force's meetings are available from the FASB, and a limited number of individuals and organizations subscribe to a service that sends them the minutes automatically. However, the minutes are not indexed, with the consequence that it is difficult to find a ruling on a particular issue without an extensive search.

In 1987, it appears that the EITF will survive because of its proven ability to act on issues far more quickly than the FASB. It is accepted by Board Members because it allows them to focus on bigger issues, and it is accepted by auditors because it gives them quick answers. Most important, the Chief Accountant's endorsement gives its work the credibility that it needs to go on into the future.

Summary

There will always be a fine balance between issuing too many and too few standards, and the members of the Financial Accounting Standards Board will always have to tread carefully. It is quite possible that the Board did issue too many pronouncements in the late 1970s and the early 1980s. Since then, it has clearly moved in the other direction, perhaps even to the extent that it may have overcompensated by providing too little authoritative guidance. This equally undesirable position might be aggravated if it turns out that the EITF is actually undermining the Board's authority by acting as a de facto authoritative body.

As is true for so many complex problems, there is no easy "one-shot" solution to the standards overload and timely guidance problems; success in coping with them will be achieved only through a careful and ongoing monitoring of the situation.

STATEMENT PREPARER PARTICIPATION VERSUS DOMINANCE

One cornerstone of the FASB standards-setting system is that improvement of financial accounting practice through changes in generally accepted accounting principles will eventually lead to a **more effective allocation** of resources in the capital markets.

Another fundamental and important purpose for GAAP is to **constrain managers** against reporting in a biased way that makes their performance or condition appear better than it actually was. This tendency is not necessarily an outgrowth of an unethical frame of mind but may be the result of a perfectly normal desire to present a good image.

Another cornerstone for the FASB's operations is its policy of having an open discussion and debate of the issues at hand. Thus, there is a due process that allows everyone to **participate** and make their views known to the Board, even if they are coming from the management that is to be constrained against bias.

But this freedom to participate also creates the significant risk that a single interest group might obtain the upper hand in the Board's deliberations and infringe on the legitimate interests of the other groups. If this situation were to arise, the purposes for having GAAP might be compromised or even completely defeated. This problem would be especially troublesome if financial statement preparers were to become the dominant group because they are the ones who are being regulated. The possibility that this **preparer dominance** problem could arise is suggested by what some observers believe has happened in other situations in which the regulated industries have taken over control of the regulatory mechanism. For example, this condition has been alleged to exist for some state public service commissions that are charged with regulating various utilities.

It is appropriate, therefore, to consider whether the FASB is about to or has already fallen under the dominance of preparers. In the eyes of some, there is evidence that the condition already exists.

From one perspective, they assert that preparers have established a very high profile in Board activities. With respect to **comment letters** received in response to discussion documents and Exposure Drafts, more usually come from preparers than from any other group. For the Defeasance project described in the Prologue, preparers sent in 38 out of 62 comment letters on the first Exposure Draft (61 percent) and 47 out of 74 on the second (64 percent). Although Board Members deny that they are persuaded by a count of the responses for or against a position, it certainly would be understandable if they were to feel overwhelmed by a large number of letters opposing a preliminary position.

Another indication of a high profile for preparers is the fact that approximately 56 percent of the Financial Accounting Foundation's **donated funds** come from "industry."[5] Again, Board Members are supposed to be immune from being swayed by this fact because they do not have any responsibilities for raising funds; however, they might be influenced by threats that a particular position on an issue would result in the elimination of donations. The potential for this susceptibility to financial pressure was described by Dr. Stephen Zeff shortly after the FASB's Rules of Procedures were amended in 1978 to give preparers more influence while the AICPA's influence was

---

[5]This category also includes an unidentified (but reportedly small) portion from banks and similar financial institutions. Because banks are both preparers and users of financial statements, a more exact determination of the percentage from preparers is difficult to make.

diminished.[6] By coincidence, Dr. Zeff was in the audience at the 1984 seminar referred to in Chapter 2 (see page 36) when the controller for Texaco threatened to eliminate his company's contribution to the Foundation if the FASB did not change its proposed pension accounting standards. Another example occurred early in the Board's deliberations of the project to revise SFAS 33. Specifically, Board Member Frank Block said (first in a closed meeting with staff members, and then in a public meeting) that many corporate donors did not like the disclosures required by the Standard and that he was inclined to think that they should be accommodated.

Another indication of dominance is the fact that four out of fifteen (27 percent) of the Foundation's Trustees come from preparer backgrounds, and it is the stated goal of the Trustees to elect a corporate executive as the sixteenth, which will give preparers 31 percent. Nine members of the Financial Accounting Standards Advisory Council are preparers (31 percent), and bankers hold another four positions (14 percent). Preparers also hold one-fourth of the seats on the Emerging Issues Task Force.

These signs of the high profile of preparers could be perceived as more ominous when they are contrasted against the evidence of the low profile that has been established by users, apart from the SEC's participation and influence. With respect to comment letters, there is a very low rate of responses from users in comparison to all those who respond. For each of the two Defeasance Exposure Drafts, only three letters were received from users, which amounted to less than 5 percent of the total. Additionally, virtually none of the Foundation's donations come from the user community, only two Trustees are connected with the user constituency, less than 10 percent of the members of FASAC represent the user community, and there are no users on the EITF.

Evidence of preparer dominance (and the consistently low level of user participation) can be seen in the **reduced level of the SEC's activism**, which was described in Chapter 5. That chapter also described the pressures that led to the compromising of the direction of the Conceptual Framework project and the Board's answer to the pension liability problem. Although the pressures came from several sources, it is accurate to state that much of their force was based on support from the preparer community.

Another sign that preparers are seeking dominance is less systematically observed, but nonetheless may show that they are gaining an upper hand. Specifically, some powerful preparers have used various media to express **severe criticisms of the FASB**. For example, Mr. Roger Smith, the Chairman of the Board of General Motors, was interviewed by a reporter from *DH+S Review,* a newsletter published by Deloitte Haskins & Sells, the Big Eight auditing firm used by General Motors. The article presented some of his views on the FASB:

---

[6]See Stephen Zeff, "The Rise of Economic Consequences," *Journal of Accountancy,* December 1978, p. 60.

"I've been a strong advocate of standards-setting in the private sector rather than in the public, and I think the SEC prefers that also," [says] Chairman Smith. . . . He adds, however, that this puts the onus on the private sector to do the job properly, and that he has been disappointed by some of the actions taken by the FASB. "I think they've issued far too many rules and have gotten away from their original charter. And I believe that it's time that they stop and take stock of what their mission is," he says.

Roger Smith very pointedly says, "I think the Board wandered away from what they should be doing by prescribing the way people should run their business rather than how business operations should be reported." Mr. Smith continues, "I believe a lot of good sensible business practice has been sacrificed by the FASB on the altar of uniformity. And, that's not right." He points to the effects of earlier foreign currency accounting standards to demonstrate how business policies were affected and to the potential effects of the introduction of current value accounting concepts and the earlier pension accounting proposals. The GM Chairman concludes, "this is one of the major reasons why the Business Roundtable and others have been urging that the Financial Accounting Foundation appoint a blue-ribbon committee to come in and take an independent look at what the mission of the FASB is and how well they're accomplishing it. I think that's an essential thing to do at this time."[7]

There are a number of strong criticisms within Smith's comments. Note, for example, how he raises the issue of whether the SEC should take over standards setting and then places the "onus" on the FASB rather than on those who participate in its processes. He also expresses value judgments when he uses words like "disappointed," "far too many," "wandered away," and "sacrificed by the FASB on the altar of uniformity." He also expresses no confidence in the competence of the FASB and the Foundation to accomplish a legitimate review; instead, he would appoint a "blue-ribbon" committee, which suggests that he does not believe that Board Members and trustees are of "blue-ribbon" caliber. It should also be noted that all the members of "the Business Roundtable" are preparers.

Criticism from the preparer community reached a new level of boldness in July 1985, when Robert W. Moore, president of the Financial Executives Institute, delivered a "position paper" to the trustees of the Financial Accounting Foundation. The paper, which was developed by a special ad hoc committee of the FEI (similar to the one proposed by Roger Smith), addressed a number of issues related to preparer participation. Two particularly significant recommendations in Moore's cover letter to Rholan Larson, President of the Foundation, were (1) that at least five of the trustees of the Foundation should come from the preparer constituency (instead of the then serving three) and (2) that "additional qualified business-experienced candidates be considered to fill the vacancies that will be created on the FASB in

---

[7]"Chairman Roger Smith Steers GM along New Avenues," *DH+S Review,* April 1, 1985, p. 2.

1985 and 1986." The subcommittee specified that two out of the three new vacancies should be filled with people who have "broad based business experience."

In developing the rationale for the recommendations, the committee rejected the FASB's most fundamental premise that the objective of financial reporting is to provide useful information to external, nonmanagement users. The committee's paper includes this statement:

> An often overlooked fact is that business people [defined by the committee as managers] are major—if not primary—users of financial statements and reports.[8]

Because of their point of view, the members of the committee did not address any comments to the problem that is created by having a regulatory authority dominated by the regulated group.

In October 1985, the Trustees appointed Art Northrop (who had retired after 40 years with IBM) as a Board Member, thereby giving preparers two seats and users none. In 1986, the Trustees made the previously mentioned commitment to electing a chief executive officer as an at-large Trustee.

With respect to the appointment of the chairman in 1986, it is unclear to the authors whether the Trustees responded to the FEI initiatives. The Trustees selected Denny Beresford after he emerged as a candidate late in the deliberations when they could not reach a consensus on any of three other leading candidates. Although his background was in auditing, Beresford is linked to the preparer constituency by the fact that he was nominated for the chairmanship by the National Association of Accountants, which is comprised of corporate accounting officials.[9] In addition, he was connected with the Financial Executives Institute through his co-authorship of a monthly column in the FEI's journal. On the other hand, a close observer characterized Beresford's actions and votes during the first year of his chairmanship as not at all reflective of preparers' views on the issues before the Board.

Preventing or Reversing the Problem

Whether preparer dominance would be a problem is, of course, a matter of one's perspective on the standards-setting process. Similarly, there are disagreements on the issue of whether dominance already exists in fact. Because at least some think there is a problem and others think there could be a problem, it is appropriate to consider the steps that might be taken to prevent its occurrence or to reverse its effects. We suggest that one or more of the following organizations or groups could take the described action.

---

[8]Financial Executives Institute, "The Business Community's Role in the Development of Accounting Standards," July 18, 1985.

[9]See Kathy Williams, "Dennis R. Beresford: New FASB Chairman," *Management Accounting,* December 1986, p. 2.

Securities and Exchange Commission. Preparer dominance could be turned aside by the SEC's adoption of a higher profile in its oversight of the FASB. By being openly supportive of efforts to initiate user-oriented reforms in financial accounting (as it was in the late 1970s), the SEC could boost the confidence of the Board Members and reduce preparer influence. For example, if the SEC had supported the FASB's pension accounting proposals in the 1982 Preliminary Views document, the Board might not have retreated as far as it did. Another measure would be the providing of detailed guidance from the Chief Accountant to the Board on how to resolve specific issues. A more extreme step would be guidance to the Trustees on who to appoint to the Board. An even more extreme step would be the contribution of funds by the SEC to the FAF. Of course, the adoption of a more active role by the SEC depends on the goals and priorities of the Commissioners and the president who appoints them.

Board Members. A critical counteractive force can be found in the personal convictions of individual Board Members that preparer dominance should be resisted. Some strength is generated for them by the institutional independence of their positions. Because only they have been given the power to vote on the issues, their determination to control the influence of preparers (or any other group) is critical.

Financial Accounting Foundation Trustees. Another important source of resistance to preparer dominance is the trustees, who have the primary task of insulating Board Members from political and economic pressure. In addition to establishing other sources of contributions and other means of assuring the financial independence of the Board, the trustees could also take an active stance in responding to criticisms from preparers and others. Further, their choices of Board Members and the selection of their own at-large members certainly affect the influence of preparers (or any other group).

Financial statement users. Highly visible participation in the Board's due process procedures by users would help counteract the influence of preparers. After all, it is users who are the most obvious beneficiaries of the FASB's efforts to reform GAAP. Nonetheless, that participation has not been forthcoming in the past, perhaps because unsophisticated users do not understand financial accounting or how they can affect the standards-setting process. Furthermore, it is quite likely that sophisticated users have private sources of information that would become worthless if more financial information were to be provided to the public. Thus, activism by the SEC may have to suffice for getting users' views known to the FASB.

Auditors. Because the credibility of the auditing profession depends on an arm's-length relationship with its clients, it must remain independent. If its independence were to be compromised or lost by having GAAP shaped under preparer control, auditors could lose their role in society. Thus, it may be in auditors' self-interest to counteract preparer dominance, perhaps through more participation in the Board's due process procedures and an increased level of donations to the Foundation.

Financial statement preparers. Paradoxically, the group that might lose the most under a condition of preparer dominance are preparers themselves. Specifically, if it were to become clear that accounting standards were continually being shaped to reflect powerful preparers' preferences rather than users' needs, direct government control would become more likely, with the ultimate result that all preparers would lose their ability to participate in the standards-setting process. Thus, it could be in their own interest to moderate any confrontational tactics.

Accounting professors. Academic accountants have been relatively ineffective in the FASB's due process procedures because they lack sufficient political and economic power to influence the outcome. However, they could counteract preparer dominance by serving as a type of "public conscience" that would describe its potential dangers to the business world and the accounting profession.

Summary

It is quite clear that preparer dominance could reduce the FASB's effectiveness as a standards-setting body. This condition could increase the likelihood that pressures will be brought to bear to give the SEC direct responsibility for standards setting. In the authors' opinion, evidence that preparers are dominating the Board is found in some of the trustees' recent actions, and the Board's decisions to back down on the Conceptual Framework, the Pensions project, the Changing Prices project, and the Cash Flows project.

As with the problems of standards overload and timely guidance, there is no "quick fix." Rather, it will take time and cooperation to develop and implement a solution. Even then, it will take a continuing commitment to prevent a recurrence of the problem.

WILL THE FASB SURVIVE?

Perhaps the ultimate question to be asked about the FASB's future is whether it **ought** to have one. Some academic accountants have argued that the capital markets are their own best regulators because providers of capital will require higher rates of return from companies that do not provide useful information to compensate for the higher risk inherent in such situations. Thus, these academics would prefer a situation in which there would be no requirements for external reporting or any standards that would specify the contents of any external reports. Other academics have argued that the ready availability of massive data processing capabilities has made regular public reporting obsolete. They suggest that corporations should make all of their accounting data available in electronic form, so users could access the parts they think are relevant and reliable instead of depending on decisions made by standards setters, auditors, and statement preparers.

While these ideas are intellectually interesting and certainly worthy of debate, the authors have concluded that they are unrealistic because they do not take into consideration the political factors that have brought the SEC and the FASB into existence and kept them operating. Thus, they believe that the responsibility placed on the FASB is legitimate and important.

The authors also conclude that the FASB has made a positive contribution to financial accounting; thus, by the linkage described in Chapter 1, there is adequate evidence to support the conclusion that the FASB contributes to the well-being of the U.S. economy and should be allowed to exist into the future.

Once it is determined that the FASB **ought** to have a future, the next question is whether it **will** have one. This question cannot be answered without first noting that the Board has the very difficult job of resolving complex and controversial issues in the midst of groups of powerful partici-pants who often have conflicting interests. Given this task and this setting, it is always possible that a few changes could bring the system down, even if the good intentions of the participants are that it continue.

Although these difficulties have existed throughout its history, the Board has been able to survive longer than the APB with a far greater influence on the practice of accounting. The FASB has achieved this record like any other survivor in **politics**: its **people** have been sensitive to the needs of their constituents and the environment, and the **process** has been sufficiently flexible to adapt to changes in those needs. If the sensitivity and the flexibility continue into the future, there is every reason to expect the FASB to continue to exist and to have a major effect on financial accounting.

SELECTED READINGS

KIRK, DONALD J. "FASB Standards: Too Many or Too Few?" *Journal of Account-ancy,* February 1983, pp. 75–80.

LARSON, RHOLAN E., and THOMAS P. KELLEY. "Differential Measurement in Ac-counting Standards: The Concept Makes Sense." *Journal of Accountancy,* No-vember 1984, pp. 78–90.

MOSSO, DAVID. "Standards Overload—No Simple Solution." *Journal of Account-ancy,* November 1983, pp. 120–38.

ROBBINS, BARRY P. "Perspectives on Tax Basis Financial Statements." *Journal of Accountancy,* August 1985, pp. 89–100.

THOMAS, BARBARA S. "Timely Guidance: What Role for the SEC and FASB?" *Financial Executive,* October 1983, pp. 34–39.

REVIEW QUESTIONS

1. Even though the FASB is not a governmental agency, how can it be argued that the setting of financial accounting standards is a public process?

2. Describe six benefits that accrue to the SEC by having the FASB set accounting standards.

3. What difficulties would have to be overcome to create a governmental agency for setting accounting standards?

4. What is standards overload? What is timely guidance? Can they both occur at the same time? Explain.

5. What problem is created for the FASB by the fact that it gets authority from the SEC, the AICPA, state boards of public accountancy, and state societies of CPAs?

6. What events contributed to the perception that standards overload existed and was the FASB's fault?

7. Are other activities subject to the possibility of standards overload? What do participants in those activities do about it?

8. What are the advantages and disadvantages of having two sets of GAAP?

9. What is the composition of the Emerging Issues Task Force? What constituent group is not directly represented?

10. Why would it be controversial to have the EITF creating GAAP?

11. What risk is created by having a due process that allows a regulated group to participate in the development of regulations? What are the advantages of this relationship?

12. What signs indicate that preparers dominate the FASB and its processes?

13. What could the SEC do to counteract dominance by preparers?

14. How are preparers benefited and threatened by their dominance of the standards-setting process?

EXERCISES

1. Assume that you are a CPA practicing as a sole practitioner with clients who are not under the regulations of the SEC. Prepare a letter to the FASB either (1) requesting it to consider separate accounting standards for your type of clients or (2) indicating why separate standards are not necessary.

2. Review *The Wall Street Journal,* the *Journal of Accountancy* and other accounting-related sources to identify corporate failures and frauds during the last several years. Determine whether the problem appeared to be a function of management, inadequate accounting standards, inadequate auditing standards, or some other factors. Do your results suggest to you that the setting of accounting standards in the private sector is not succeeding?

NAME INDEX

SUBJECT INDEX